LOOKING FOR UTOPIA

A Memoir

LOOKING FOR UTOPIA

A Memoir

Bertram Silverman

FCP

Full Court Press
Englewood Cliffs, New Jersey

First Edition

Copyright © 2024 by Bertram Silverman

Published in the United States of America
by Full Court Press, 601 Palisade Avenue,
Englewood Cliffs, NJ 07632
fullcourtpress.com

ISBN 978-1-953728-24-1
Library of Congress Control No. 2024900713

Editing and book design by Barry Sheinkopf

TO ALICE
with love

Table of Contents

INTRODUCTION

SOMETHING IS MISSING. The utopian hopes and dreams of my youth have faded. Stripped of anticipation, a sense of foreboding unsettles my daily routines. I try to find my footing in an absurd world and search for signs of meaning and direction to the twisted turns of history that my generation has witnessed. I know only too well that melancholy is the flip side of hope, and struggle to avoid its grip. I hide these thoughts from friends and attempt to project a sunny disposition.

I need to imagine some end to life that transcends my tiny allotment of time and space. But I find it difficult to dream in a world filled with nightmarish violence; a time in America when, as the historian Andrew Delbanco observed, "hope has narrowed to the vanishing point of the self" as so many of the world's dispossessed search frantically and dangerously for a sense of identity and belonging. And yet I can't let go. I need to know how to dream in a world of diminishing expectations.

I realize as I write these words how deeply my utopian disposition remains a part of who I am. Is this, as Freud believed, simply an infantile need for motherly connection? Or is it a human need to want to be a part of something larger than oneself? The symptoms are clear. Play John Lennon singing "Imagine," and I become teary-eyed. Frank Sinatra's rendition of "Yesterday" also invokes feelings of something lost and irretrievable. I have little control over these feelings. They are simply there.

On the face of it, the songs are quite different, yet they touch on two elements of utopian longing. "Yesterday" romanticizes the past and seeks to capture feelings of lost innocence. "Imagine" asks us to dream of possibilities of an ideal world, of a heaven on earth, a utopia. Still, nostalgic and utopian yearnings do have something in common. They capture a search for belonging, a place to feel at home in the relentless disruption of modern life. But utopian hope touches something more. It is also a search for a transcendent story to help us navigate through life's inevitable terminus and to abate fearful feelings of loneliness.

I realize that my desire to be part of a community that shares my values, and my dreams of a better world, must be carefully distinguished. The Lebanese-born French writer Anin Maalouf clarifies these different yearnings. "On the one hand, he writes, "there is the desire for a vision of the world that transcends our existence with its suffering and disappointments and gives meaning—even if only an illusory one—to life and death." This spiritual need draws on our moral imagination and seeks to identify the commonalities of the human condition. On the other hand, Maalouf suggests, "There is the need felt by every individual, to feel part of a community which accepts and recognizes him and within which he can be understood easily." My Israeli cousin Uri while dismayed by the anti-democratic turn in Israel, insists that he could never leave Israel because it's the only place he can speak a language without an accent.

I have learned that the search for belonging must be kept apart from the spiritual need for some transcendent vision. I have lived long enough to witness how violence erupts when a transcendent vision, religious or secular, merges with the need to belong to a national or religious community. The 20th century is replete with examples of how beliefs in abstract humanism have coexisted with contempt for real human beings. As the poet G. K. Chesterton exclaimed, "The villas and chapels where / I learned with little labor/The way to love my fellow man / And hate my neighbor."

My rational self accepts such sentiments and asks whether I can still have utopian dreams? The question makes me uneasy. My utopian impulses rely on my imagination. They draw deeply on my ethical and moral sentiments. I am therefore, constantly questioning the inequalities and injustices that divide communities and undermine the creation of a more cooperative commonwealth. I cannot accept the world as it is and so like Sisyphus I continue to hold on to my utopian ideals while my more rational self is filled with doubts. Are my dreams an illusion designed to ease my anxiety about death? Perhaps such doubts are the very nature of moral longings and will always be a part of who I am.

Lennon's call to "Imagine" suggests that I am not alone. Utopian hope inspires because it speaks not about politics or social movements but to our moral imagination. It is part of our ethical compass that evaluates and guides us through life's travails. I take comfort from the social critic Irving Howe's words that our conception of what is good and what is right can never condescend to what is, because reality is an unfolding human project. Utopian hope rejects the mistaken belief that what is will be with us tomorrow. Against the increasingly despairing view that there are no longer any alternatives to modern capitalism, Howe argues that utopian hope offers an appreciation of history's surprises and possibilities. Such hope, he argues, provides no practical guide to the current state of affairs. Its practicality lies in yearning for something different as against "acquiescing in the given simply because it is here." I would add that the critical eye of the dreamer provides an impulse to change and reform what is otherwise considered inevitable or natural.

And yet I hesitate to speak openly about my utopian disposition. Idealistic visions, hopes, and desires for social innovation are no longer fashionable and are often seen as dangerous illusions that set off memories of violence and totalitarian nightmares. To be associated with such sentiments reflects badly on one's character and one's capacity for a more mature and intelligent understanding of the human condition.

The responses of many of my friends reflect the mood of our times. The question begins innocently enough. "So, tell me what you're working on these days," or "What are you doing with your time now that you've retired?"

I answer with some hesitancy and embarrassment, "I'm writing an essay on my search for utopia."

There's a long pause and then the usual innocuous phrase, "That's interesting. I didn't know you're still into that stuff."

Doris, a close friend of my wife, smiles and somewhat mockingly asks, "Do you still believe in all that wishful thinking?" Cynicism best describes her current mood. It is a temperament widely shared. Mistrust is a key element of this disposition: mistrust of visions, of a better future, of science, of reason, of modernity. It is reflected in the paintings of her deceased husband, a brilliant artist whose satirical and dystopian images explore the farcicality of the human condition. Doris shares this sense of absurdity. She has a keen eye for style and a nuanced understanding of changing consumer fashions. She is not interested in probing too deeply and analytically beyond what she cannot observe. Her preoccupation with appearances is part of her knowing sense that life is short, fragile, and unpredictable and is a game that should be played as much as possible with humor and enjoyment. She touches something in me that also wants to take life less seriously and find pleasures in the here and now.

My friend Gene Goodheart, a distinguished professor of literature, now gone, felt somewhat more threatened by my project. He shared my history and struggled with the same youthful dreams of reconciling the world he hoped for with the one in which he lived. I think he believed I never fully absorbed the proper lessons from those shared experiences. We attended the same "shuleh," an after-school program where we studied Yiddish, learned about Jewish history and culture, and studied a communist version of Marxism. Our parents were deeply devoted to Jewish culture and in our youth looked to the Soviet Union as the hope for a communist utopia. Gene and I recited the poems of the Jewish poet Itzik Feffer, praising Stalin and the Soviet Union, who with other prominent Jewish intellectuals and professionals became victims of Stalinist terror.

Gene and I shared the same code words and could cut to the cusp of an argument about familiar questions. You cannot, he reminded me, so easily separate utopian dreams from nostalgic longing. Utopian visions are always embedded in romantic perceptions of some lost innocence and simpler existence. Marxist images of a communist utopia were, he insisted, an idealized version of primitive communism.

"I know," I countered, "hunter in the morning, fisherman in the afternoon and critical critic after supper. . . ."

But, he persisted, these are not innocent images of an earlier state of human existence but dangerous illusions that when pursued can explode into totalitarian nightmares. I shared with Gene an admiration of Yeats' lines, "We fed the heart on fantasy / the heart grew brutal on the fare."

I still feel the tension in my body from when I resisted Gene's admonitions to beware of utopian dreams. I respond cautiously. I'm not fully convinced of my argument. I too am deeply wounded by the failure of our youthful dreams. The totalitarian nightmares of Nazi Germany and the Soviet Union, I counter, do not mean that we should discard our dreams of a more cooperative and civically engaged society where the power of money no longer dominates all spheres of life. The ideals of social justice are not, as Hayek would have it, a slippery slope to serfdom. No doctrine, secular or religious, has a monopoly on fanaticism. They all have blood on their hands. Rather, the historical circumstances in which liberalism, socialism, nationalism, and religion live reveal their liberating, violent, or pacific tendencies. But how do I keep dreaming under those circumstances? I end my conversation with Gene by asking if we can still learn to dream. It's a question that has haunted my life.

Chapter 1

LEARNING TO DREAM

N BARBARA KINGSOLVER'S NOVEL *Animal Farm,* a woman asks her lover, "Didn't you ever dream you could fly?" He answers, "Not when I was sorting pecans all day." Really, she persists, "Didn't you ever fly in your dreams?" He replies, "Only when I was close to flying in real life. . . . Your dreams, what you hope for and all that, it's not separated from your life. It grows right out of it."

When I read these lines, memories of my father resurface. My father was not a dreamer. Despite the harshness of his early life experiences, he remained deeply wedded to the here and now. He lived in the present, resigned to the cards life had dealt him. It was not from him that I learned to dream of a brighter future. I rarely saw him when I was child. During the Great Depression he found a job as a grocery clerk in a small Harlem supermarket and worked there for the remainder of his working life even though he was a skilled watchmaker. My mother constantly reminded us that it was his lack of ambition that wedded him to a low-wage job and long working hours.

Through my early childhood I rarely saw him. He left our small apartment in the Bronx from Monday through Saturday at six in the morning and did not return until eight at night. He worked half a day on Sunday. Through most of this period he remained a man of mystery, a figure of great authority and strength. My mother reinforced this image by constantly warning that, unless we behaved, our father would punish us when he came home.

But my twin sister and I learned to ignore such threats. By the time we reached our eighth birthday, his store was unionized, and his working hours were reduced. We then saw him more often and discovered a gentle and fun-loving man who, unlike our mother, rarely raised his voice in anger. Since we saw him during dinner and playtime, we joyfully anticipated his return from work. Sundays were special occasions. Our family often spent the day enjoying simple pleasures. When the weather was warm and sunny, we would walk and boat in Bronx Park. On special occasions we would take a train to Manhattan to see a movie at Radio City Music Hall or the Roxy and after the show eat at the automat where, with five nickels, I could buy whatever I liked to eat.

As the years passed, I began to wonder why he didn't leave his Harlem job. He came to America trained as a skilled watchmaker and owned a complete set of tools to practice his craft. Even during the Second World War, when much better employment opportunities were available, he refused to leave his job. Whatever his reasons he seemed content with his lot, even grateful for what he had. He lived neither in the past nor for the future. He never wanted to dig too deeply into the choices he made in his life. When I questioned him about his youthful experiences in Pinsk, he would shrug and say, "What is there to tell, life was very hard then, but that's over. Things are much better now." When I persisted, he would simply say, "Who remembers, it was so long ago." My father was a simple man who never asked much of life.

Did my father ever dream he could fly? There was one moment. I remember it vividly. We had just returned from visiting the 1939 World's Fair. We rode on a train that took us into an imagined future world. Responding to our excitement over the novelty and promise of things to come, he laughed and said with a twinkle in his eye, "All of us will soon be able to fly. We'll have motors strapped to our backs, and we will fly just like birds."

"Wow," I said, "do you think that will really happen?"

"Of course," he said, "and sooner than you think."

But those were rare occasions. My father lived in the present. He accepted the hardness of life and appreciated the simple pleasures that life afforded, shrugging off my mother's constant complaint that he lacked ambition. He was a quiet man who kept his feelings to himself. And yet he found his own way to escape the routines of work and my mother's disapproving gaze.

Music provided a path that stirred his imagination. I would often find him alone, listening to classical, popular, and folk music, especially Yiddish songs that captured the lost world of Jewish immigrants and their longings. He had a beautiful voice and would often sing Yiddish and English lullabies that still move me when I hear them.

In the end music provided the recognition and self-esteem that Mom thought he would never achieve. I remember traveling to South Beach, Miami, where they lived after my father retired, and asking my mother where Pop was. Somewhat dismissively, she replied, "He's singing at some concert near the beach."

Curious, I walked to the beach, wondering what he was doing. I finally found him standing on a stage, singing to more than two hundred retired Jewish women and men who, like my father, had made the long journey from the Pale to the small shops and factories of New York and finally to Miami Beach, where they recreated a new Jewish settlement.

He was singing some of the songs he had learned from Sidor Belarsky's recordings of Yiddish ballads. In a clear and melodious voice, he captured feelings of a lost world that resonated among his audience. To my surprise many of the elderly Jews were weeping. I understood at that moment that my father had found something deep within himself that he could share with others. When he finished, the audience rose, giving him a standing ovation. He simply smiled and sat down.

Overcome by what I had seen, I told him how much I enjoyed his performance and asked if he was anxious singing before such a large audience. "Why should I be nervous?" he responded. "I'm just singing songs I love to people I know." My father's capacity to live in the moment, his acceptance of himself, put a somewhat different face on what my mother had interpreted as complacency and lack of ambition. After becoming well known within his community, and even when people began calling him the Jewish Frank

Sinatra, he never sought to promote himself or exhibit any sign of self-importance. Did my father dream? Perhaps, but only when he was singing.

Unlike my father, my mother lived for the future. If he found gratification in the simple pleasures life offered, Mom experienced few joys in the burdens of raising twins on my father's meager wages. And so she invented her own reality to help overcome the burdens of mothering and her feelings of loneliness and insignificance. It was in her dreams that she found a way of rising above her immediate circumstances to find something in herself that she could honor.

Mom wanted a husband who could share her visions of a better life, not only for herself but for the world at large. Someone who could understand her unfulfilled yearnings and could ease the anxieties that troubled her soul. My father could not give her what she wanted because he did not understand what she needed. The more she complained about his passivity, the more he withdrew into his private thoughts. Even when she could no longer cope with her anxieties and needed hospitalization, Pop was incapable of understanding the level of her despair or the causes of her psychological distress.

So she turned to her children, with whom she shared her dreams and desires as well as her anxieties and discontents. I was more fortunate than my sister, who could not so easily resist absorbing the demons buried deeply in my mother's breasts. Gender must have played a role in this unfair transference of our mother's anxieties. Perhaps my sister tended to identify more with our mother while I sought separation to assert my independence. Whatever the reason, I was given greater opportunities to spend time away from my mother's grasp.

My sister did not have such advantages. She never left my mother's side and consequently became more attuned to her changing moods and her constant complaints about life's troubles. To my sister, Mom's stories of surviving the terror of the First World War, the incarceration in a German prison camp, and the upheaval of emigration only confirmed her anxiety that Mom might abandon her. These fears were confirmed when Mom irrationally threatened to leave us when we misbehaved.

As a boy I took advantage of opportunities to explore the world beyond my mother's grasp. At an early age the street outside our small apartment became a playground where I formed friendships, learned new games, and discovered an awakening sexuality. I was rather good at sports and soon found myself playing stickball, basketball, and touch football with the older boys on our block. Parents organized stickball tournaments against other neighborhood teams. Scoreboards were displayed in front of the candy store on our block. The fathers of some my teammates placed small wagers on our team. I felt that our honor was at stake when the game began. I still remember the shame I felt after a high-spinning Spaulding popped out of my glove and the tying and winning runs of the opposing team crossed home plate. Terrified and too ashamed to face my friends and their fathers, I quickly ran home. I did not leave my apartment until a few friends came by and told me that it was okay to come down to play.

Despite these moments of humiliation that forced me to seek my mother's protection, I found the freedom of the streets empowering and exciting. There was so much to explore, so much to discover beyond the confines of my small apartment. But I also learned, while walking to Bathgate Avenue with my mother and sister, that I needed to be very careful how I expressed my new sense of autonomy.

Bathgate Avenue was quite a distance from our apartment. I had never ventured there on my own. Mom would take us whenever she wanted to buy clothing or some household item. One early winter day five months after my eighth birthday, walking with my mother and sister to Bathgate Avenue, I drifted off on my own, looking at the windows of the many stores that lined Tremont Avenue. My mother with my sister in tow, thinking I was following her, walked into a store. As soon as I turned from gazing in the window of a toy store, I realized that Mom was no longer in sight. I panicked, not knowing what to do. I ran up the block, anxiously searching for her. I was on the verge of crying but suddenly realized I wasn't lost. I could find my way home and wait for her there. I began running carefully, observing all the traffic signals. Before long I found my way back and immediately started playing with my friends. I still felt anxious about being separated from my mother but proud of finding my own way home.

It was not long before I saw my mother and sister walking quickly toward me. I smiled as they approached, certain that she would be delighted to see me. The anger and anguish on her face soon dispelled such hopes. She pulled me toward her and screamed, "How could you *do* this to me?" She ripped off my hat and began hitting me on my head. Stunned, I was unable to move. Blood began to flow down my face. In her rage my mother had forgotten that my cap had a metal clasp. When she realized what had happened, she quickly stopped and hugged me, saying she hit me because she loved me. I was confused but relieved she was no longer angry. Separating from my mother's watchful eyes would continue to be an important part of my struggle for independence.

As a boy I was the favored child. Mom wanted me to be someone she imagined she could have been. She filled my imagination with inspirational stories of heroic figures and events that she thought would serve as guides towards a more meaningful life. They were a confusing array of norms and values that she applied on different occasions and for different purposes.

She valued education but warned, when I challenged her knowledge, that wisdom came from the richness of a life lived and not only from reading books. It was her constant reminder that my educational achievements could never compete with her worldly experiences. She wanted me to be motivated by moral rather than material interest, but she also wanted me to enjoy the economic rewards and status that a professional life would bring. And so she wanted me to be a diligent student who performed well in school, but cautioned that too much studying would dull my enjoyment of life.

Despite these conflicting instructions, Mom had one overriding moral message. To be a good person meant caring more about others than about your own personal gain. To help someone in need was the highest of callings. When she wanted to dismiss someone out of hand she would say with contempt, "She is not a good person, she thinks only about herself." There were very few who could measure up to Mom's standards of conduct.

I grew up thinking about the larger scheme of things often failing to recognize what my father knew: the importance of the simple pleasures of life. I think he would have appreciated the socialist playwright Sean O'Casey's celebration of the sweetness of everyday life:

> What time has been wasted during man's destiny in the struggle to decide what man's next world will be like! The keener the effort to find out the less he knows about the present one he lived in. The one lovely world he knew that gave him all he was, according to preacher and prelate, the one to be least in his thoughts. . . . Oh, we have had enough of the abuse of this fair earth! It is no sad truth that this should be our home. Were it but to give us simple shelter, simple clothing, simple food, adding the lily and the rose, the apple, and the peas, it would be a fit home for mortal or immortal men.

Mom never accepted the world as it is. She would not have rejected O'Casey's description of a world of more modest strivings, but she would have asked how, without a vision of something better, could humanity find "a fit home for mortal and immortal men." I don't think she felt good enough about herself to ever imagine living only in the present. It was in her dreams that she found a place where she could be honored and respected. She never had many close friends to whom she could turn. Her sharply critical voice hid a fragile soul. I had difficulty reconciling how she could be so assertive, rising at a meeting to challenge a speaker, rushing to my school to defend me against a perceived injustice, and yet be so vulnerable.

Mom took pride in my efforts to engage in conversations about worldly events. She saw in my achievements a way of compensating for life's disappointments. But there is a cost for such adorations. I came to believe that her love depended on my accomplishments. I remember vividly the moment when I fully understood that heavy burden. I had just successfully defended my doctoral dissertation at Columbia University. Walking down the stairs outside the small seminar room where the examination had taken place, I shouted to a friend, "That was for Mom!" as if I could now free myself from her presence. At that moment I realized that my mother's hopes and yearnings had become an important part of my own dreams and aspirations. I still wonder if it is possible to be a good person and not be engaged in doing something to improve the lives of the less fortunate.

At some point a child needs some assurances about the future, some transcendent feeling about life's ending, an answer to Peggy Lee's lament, "Is that all there is?" I don't know exactly when I first began to struggle with the angst about death. But the full realization of my mortality struck like a thunderbolt. I remember the moment vividly. I was only eight; when walking in Bronx Park on a summer evening, I thought I saw someone perched in a tree. Whatever it was disappeared as I strained to make it out. My imagination quickly took over. Did I just see an angel, or was that God? How could that be? I had been told there was no God. I moved on. I could not get the image of God descending from a tree out of my mind. I tried desperately to shake off my anxiety: "No, it isn't real." My thoughts kept spinning. But if there is no God, what happens after I die? I felt abandoned and alone. Images of being buried alive increased my sense of despair. I needed to be reassured.

I never shared this experience with my parents or even with my closest friends. I was too ashamed. I thought they would laugh at my foolish behavior. My neighborhood friends, mostly Jews and a few Catholics, had religion to help them deal with mortality. My parents had given me their own version of transcendence: a vision of a better world, something called socialism. Each of us in our lifetime could participate in achieving that bright future. We never died because we all were part of that long journey. Secretly I thought my believing friends had the better story. They could disappear on Saturday or Sunday to find solace in their prayers, where they could reaffirm their faith in God and a life ever after.

Everyone on our block knew I was different and even strange. On Saturday orthodox Jews would sometimes ask me to light their stoves and even give me a penny or two. For them I was the "Shabbos goy." I can understand their mistake. I ate bread on Passover, sometimes in full view of my friends, and I never fasted on Yom Kippur. Yet while I did not set foot in synagogue until I was a young man, none of my friends ever doubted I was Jewish. I spoke Yiddish at home and was learning to write and read it. My neighbors knew I disappeared most afternoons to go to a Jewish school. My friends only questioned how I could be a Jew and not a believer. I did not understand at that time that I was in fact a Jew and a believer. Socialism or some utopian idea of the future had become my religion—my way of dealing with the question, "Is that all there is"? If my friends had God, I had faith in some radiant future. The fact that I thought I would see this Promised Land gave me some consolation. But to the question of what happens after death Mom could only offer some vague idea of being part of nature's grand scheme, certainly not enough to ease my fears.

If socialism did not protect me from the fear of death, it did help me overcome the anxieties of everyday life. You would think that, growing up during the Great Depression and the Second World War, a child's world would be darkened by fears of impending disaster. Not me. Bad times were like a dark winter soon to be followed by the light of spring. For Mom the past and the present were passages to a bright new future. Even in their old age Mom and Pop would sing, *"Jung is yedder yedder einner ver er vil nor, yorren hubben kein bedeit, jung is jedder jedder einer ver er vil nor en a neier freier zeit."* (Everyone is young if they wish to be, years don't matter. Everyone will be young in a newer and freer time.)

Even today the anticipation of spring lifts my spirits and ignites hope of new beginnings and possibilities. As a college student I accepted my left-leaning English professor's dismissal of T. S. Eliot's famous line, "April is the cruelest month," as an indication of Eliot's misguided conservatism. Only later did I recognize in Eliot's line a wonderful way of expressing my own disappointment with unrealized promises of sunny days.

And so I have no doubt about the origins of my utopian disposition. It was my mother's gift, a legacy of her journey through the turbulent years of the twentieth century. Born in 1897 in Pinsk, a town located in what is now Belarus, she experienced the turmoil of the First World War, the Russian Revolution, and the trials of emigration to America in 1921. Her father, a respected rabbi, died when she was very young. My grandmother, overwhelmed by the burden of raising six children at a time of deprivation and war, turned to her only daughter to take charge of family responsibilities. Those calamitous events that marked the beginning of the twentieth century left an indelible imprint on her view of history.

I learned about Mom's past through stories she never tired of telling. In these tales she found a way of inventing herself as a heroic figure, a survivor who had overcome immense hardships. She told us how she challenged gender prejudice to win a scholarship to a *gymnasium*. She told us how she used her education to help her family survive internment in a German refugee camp during the First World War.

But the most important lesson that she tried to convey was that, despite all her suffering, she had witnessed the birth of a new society, a new world that would finally end the poverty and ignorance that had engulfed her childhood. In a hushed voice she spoke about hearing an inspiring speech by Trotsky calling on workers and peasants to join the Russian Revolution. She recalled encounters with Russian soldiers, emphasizing how different they were from their anti-Semitic and plundering Polish and German counterparts. She would then sigh and recount how a Russian soldier helped her family and told her of his dreams of building a new society. At this point in her story, she would smile and say, "Oh, there is so much to tell." I would beg her to continue. She seemed to be omitting the most interesting part of the story—I thought perhaps a romantic encounter. But she would just sigh and say, "I could write a book."

She came to New York speaking Yiddish, Russian, Polish, and German but not English. She was a stranger looking for a homeland where she could truly belong. But she never could find a place in the American Dream. She remained an outsider in her adopted country. She scorned its culture of economic materialism and individualism, which she identified as selfishness. She rejected ideas of assimilation, arguing that a good society would help nurture the Jewish cultural heritage that defined the core of her identity.

But her kind of Jewishness isolated her from most Jews in our neighborhood. While my mother spoke proudly of my grandfather's religious learning and how religious traditions sometimes encouraged greater sympathy for the poor, she ridiculed the ways religious beliefs deflected our understanding of the real causes of poverty. She would have approved of Marx's statement that "religion in the sigh of the oppressed creature, the heart of a heartless world, just as it is the spirit of an unspiritual condition. It is the opium of the people." We never attended synagogue, yet she managed to infuse in me a secular Jewish identity with its own spiritual and romantic yearnings.

She could speak with personal authority about a radically changing world. After all, she had moved from an impoverished rural Jewish community living in a small cottage without running water or an inside toilet to New York, where inside plumbing, the radio, subways, and automobiles transformed the experiences of her youth. She had witnessed the plunder and turmoil of the First World War and the Russian Revolution and its promise of a new and glorious future. Even her difficult journey to New York reinforced her anticipation of new possibilities.

A beloved older brother, who had provided the assistance and money that made it possible for her to attend the *gymnasium*, had been denied entry into the United States and had settled in London. Mom arranged to travel on a ship that stopped in London, permitting her to spend a day with her brother before departing for New York City. When the ship arrived, she looked for him on the dock, but he did not appear. In desperation she quickly wrote a note to him and gave it to a disembarking passenger. She lay sobbing on the bed, telling her mother that all their efforts had been in vain.

At this point in her story, Mom would pause and say she heard the voice of her brother Harry saying, *"Vehn nit, mein liber schvester, ich bin doh."* (Don't cry, my dear sister, I am here). They spent the rest of the night talking about their dreams and hopes. She would never tire of retelling the story, and in each telling I could hear the underlying message: never give up hope; everything is possible.

In her mind Harry was more than a physical presence. He represented the idealized family she never had and would never find. She never saw Harry again after that extraordinary night on that boat bound for New York. They corresponded and she dutifully sent him care packages during the Second World War. At the time of the London blitz there was talk of having his son live with us. She often spoke of traveling to London, but she waited too long. Was she afraid that the real Harry would not live up to her expectations? She would not have been disappointed. I did see my uncle Harry before he died. As I listened to the stories and his unfulfilled dreams, I heard my mother's voice.

Mom sought ways of passing on her Jewish cultural traditions and her dreams of a brighter future. She enrolled us in a secular Jewish after-school program associated with Jewish People's Fraternal Order, a branch of the communist-led International Worker's Order. It was not the only secular Jewish school we could have attended. Jewish socialists and liberals developed their own schools and cultural organizations. What distinguished our program from the others was its support of Soviet communism.

Another important difference was the IWO's efforts to organize members based on their ethnicity and race. As a teenager I attended meetings designed to bridge ethnic differences by participating in cultural and social activities of other ethnic groups. I learned that I could be a Jew and still feel a connection to the songs, dance, theater, and poetry of other ethnic and racial groups.

Mom discovered Jewish communist cultural groups soon after coming to New York. Walking home from her work in a garment factory in 1922, she bought the first edition of the Yiddish daily, the *Morgen Freiheit*. Through their reporting she discovered a Jewish community that shared her values and beliefs. Mom never joined the Communist Party, but she actively participated in Jewish reading circles, choral groups, and summer camps closely associated with it.

After their marriage she introduced my father to those groups in the hope he would become politically engaged. While he enjoyed the social and cultural interactions, he detached himself from the passionate debates and petty conflicts that small political groups often inspire. Mom never realized that this may have been one of the reasons people liked him so much. She remained a loyal reader of the *Freiheit* even after it broke with the Communist Party in 1956.

The shuleh introduced me both to Yiddish culture and communist politics. As an after-school program designed to follow us through our public-school education, it was divided into elementary (shuleh), middle (mittel shuleh) and advanced courses (hecher cursin). Most of my friends also spent part of the summer months at Camp Kinderland, a more intense extension of the shuleh experience.

My parents could not afford to send us to Camp Kinderland. Instead, my sister and I spent a few weeks each summer with my aunt and uncle in a worker's community built by the International Ladies Garment Workers' Union in Homestead, New Jersey, renamed "Roosevelt" after the war. It was there that I became aware of the bitter divisions among socialist Jews who sang the same Jewish songs but could not reconcile their different views of the Soviet Union. I didn't understand why Mom was so dismissive of my uncle and aunt's politics. We seemed to share so much. I remember the campfires where we would join in singing Yiddish and union songs. We seemed so close politically, sharing a commitment to Roosevelt's political agenda. I would soon learn how political differences could sharply divide relatives and friends who had so much in common.

I was seven years old when I began my Yiddish socialist education in I. L. Peretz Shuleh #16. Mom wanted me to spend less unsupervised time on the streets. But more importantly, she believed that shuleh provided the best way to pass on her values and cultural traditions. I already felt Jewish in so many ways. I had ingested the intonations of my mother's voice when she spoke of lost opportunities, trials of dislocation, and hopes for the future as well as the Yiddish songs my father sang to me as child that tied Yiddishkeit to parental love.

The world we inhabited reinforced our Jewish identity. The stores that lined the streets of Tremont Avenue and 180th street catered to the tastes and traditions of their Jewish customers. While a few Italian families lived on our block, a clear cultural boundary separated the Italian community of Arthur Avenue from the Jewish neighborhood of my youth.

Shuleh cultivated a secular Jewish identity that clashed with my religious Jewish friends' understanding of what it meant to be Jewish. Just a few blocks from my apartment, shuleh was inconspicuously located in a loft above a butcher and bakery store. There were two small classrooms attached to a larger open space used by parents for meetings, lectures, and cultural events. Our teacher, Chaver (comrade) Gellman, spoke to us in a cultivated Yiddish. His soft voice and gentle manner were welcoming and protective. That I called him "chaver" suggested an intimacy I never experienced in public school.

At first, I resisted going because shuleh competed with the time I spent playing with my friends. Shuleh also interfered with listening to the Lone Ranger and Jack Armstrong, the All-American Boy. Those icons of American popular culture fed my heroic fantasies of triumphing over evil and my childhood fantasies of saving my parents from some impending disaster. But shuleh also provided a refuge from the impersonal and often frightening world of public school.

I still recall the antiseptic smell and forbidding coldness of PS 67. Our teachers were mainly Irish Catholic white women whose stern voices and detachment reenforced an environment designed to ensure discipline and proper behavior. In elementary school I quickly learned about the costs of misbehaving, the humiliation of failing, and the rewards of success.

I remember a particularly painful and mortifying experience when my classmates and I anxiously awaited the arrival of our new teacher. "It's Dynamite Johnson," someone whispered. Oh, my God, I thought—this must be bad. In a menacing voice Miss Johnson told us to be still and take our assigned seats. Loaded down with our new books I quickly found my seat and hurriedly placed them in a space under my desk. The books fell to the floor with a loud bang. Miss Johnson looked menacingly in my direction. In a panic I quickly picked them up and placed them under my desk. Again, they fell with a loud thud. I could hear children laughing. Miss Johnson came running down the aisle, pulled me up from my seat, and slapped me sharply across my face. In a state of shock I shouted, "I think the desk is broken." Looking at it, Miss Johnson realized her error, and she quickly changed her demeanor. Holding me in her arms, she smiled, turning to the class, and whispered, "Isn't he a brave boy? He didn't even cry." To be called courageous by Dynamite Johnson made me feel important, but what remains embedded in my memory is my outrage at her unrestrained use of power.

From the beginning public school taught me about the humiliation of failure. The first day of the new school year was the time when we were given our new class assignments. I sat with my first-grade classmates, anxiously wondering whether I would be placed in the bright, middling, or stupid class. Miss Baker, our first-grade teacher, began reading the roll. Four names were called including that of my twin sister, who was escorted to her new class. My heart sank as Miss Baker began reading the names of the middle group. Students all around me rose as their names were called. When the final name was read, a sinking feeling of humiliation gripped me. When my name was finally called, I marched out of the room, head bowed, with two other students to class 2-2, marked as one of the three dumb students.

Yes, it was an error. Outraged, my immigrant mother marched me to school the next day, and I was reunited with my sister. But the damage was done. I would never forget that burning moment of shame. I learned very early in my life, not only the consequence of failure, but also how it can be arbitrarily inflicted. Learning discipline, respecting authority, competing for success—those were some of the values we were expected to learn in preparation for our future roles as workers and citizens. I discovered later that more privileged students attending private schools followed a different script, one that encouraged creativity and individual initiative.

In the I. L. Peretz shuleh I learned to dream in ways that were unimaginable in public school. I was taught to desire but to aspire in a different way. Shuleh opened my mind to visions of a more humane society where the power of money over the lives of people would end and a new, more cooperative socialist society would emerge. In fact, we were taught that such a society was being built in the Soviet Union. How different those childhood visions were from the stereotype of the Jew using money to control and corrupt our society. It was a time when such beliefs were on the rise in Europe as well as in America.

All of us live with certain values that we have acquired from our parents and the world they inhabited. Of course, as Irving Howe has written, "We cannot be our fathers, we cannot live like our mothers, but we look to those experiences to ask the most fundamental questions. What kind of life should we lead? What norms should we use to make judgments about the meaning of a 'good life'?" The person I have become, what I consider good and what I consider bad, is deeply rooted in my secular Jewish upbringing. Richard Rorty correctly notes that all beliefs central to a person's sense of self are so because their presence or absence serves as a guide for distinguishing good people from bad people, the type of person one strives to be from the sort one does not want to be. Shuleh introduced me to larger social and political visions of the good connected to a particular secular Jewish tradition.

The code of *menschlichkeit* captures the values of my secular Jewish upbringing. The word embodies a rich and complicated ethic that lies at the heart of my utopian disposition. No one has better captured its essence than Irving Howe. Embedded in the code of menschlichkeit, he writes, "is a readiness to live for ideals beyond the clamor of self, a sense of plebian fraternity, an ability to forge a community of moral order even while remaining subject to a society of social disorder, and a persuasion that human existence is a deeply serious matter for which all of us are finally accountable."

Howe's words touch the deep roots of my utopian hopes. I often wonder how much of my secular Jewish values has been passed on to my children. Not too long ago I asked my daughters a question the philosopher Isaiah Berlin posed to a Jewish friend. "Suppose you had an Aladdin's lamp. You rub it, and all the Jews in the world would turn into happy Danes. Would you do it?" While I believed they would not rub the lamp, I was struck by the similarity of their responses. They all associated their Jewish identity with family, with feelings of belonging, but most significantly with values of empathy and justice. The buds of menschlichkeit were clearly visible in my children's values. But I wonder whether those values still inspire the passions I felt in my youth, when dreaming of new ways of living still flourished.

In shuleh we ingested a particular version Jewishness that encouraged pride in our history and culture; a Jewish identity that also enabled us to appreciate what we shared with other ethnic and racial groups. Unlike religious Jews, we did not believe we were a chosen people or in the coming of a messiah. We were taught the difference between ethnic pride and ethnic superiority, and between nationalism and patriotism: a Jewish identity that respected the diversity and richness of different cultures and nationalities.

Our teachers stressed the role that people played in making their own history. From the time of Moses and the Maccabees up to the pogroms and the hardships of migration to contemporary efforts to achieve greater equality and freedom, we learned that the path to liberation could only be achieved through resistance and struggle. We read selections from the classics of Jewish literature that included Mendele Moicher Sforim, I. L. Peretz, and Sholem Aleichem.

Peretz's story "Bontche Shveig" touched me in a special way. It told the story of a simple man who accepted a life of misery and poverty without complaint or resistance. Even when he was welcomed into heaven and God told him he could now have anything that was rightfully his, Bontche could only meekly ask for a fresh roll and butter. I read the story of Bontche at my father's gravesite as a tribute to his goodness but also as a cautionary tale about how poverty can induce complacency, not resistance to social ills of capitalism.

For religious Jews the messianic impulse meant waiting patiently for some miracle of deliverance. Not us. We were taught that history would vindicate our dreams. Even when we learned of the horrors of the Holocaust, we sang in defiance of death Hirsh Glick's hymn "Zog Nit Keinmal Az Du Geist Dem Leztin Weg." (Never say that this is the end of the journey). Hope, in this view, is not passive but is built on a readiness to engage the world and fight for one's beliefs. I remember at the age of twelve the thrill I felt while playing the role of a labor organizer in Jacob Schaefer's play *A Bund Mit a Shtazker* (A union and a strike), exhorting workers to fight against their oppressive working conditions.

The worker was the central actor in our vision of a better world. Our teachers glamorized stories of workers struggling against their bosses. We used the words "worker" and "people" interchangeably. In the populist American tradition of Walt Whitman's "Ode to Occupations" and Carl Sandberg's "The People, Yes," we were taught that the worker's fight for social and economic rights was the primary means of achieving a more just and equal society. When we were older, Marxism revealed more formally why the worker played such a central role in the forward march of history.

Jewish poverty and suffering stand out as another major theme in the Jewish experience. It was as if understanding Jewish suffering provided a deeper understanding of the human condition and possibilities of redemption. Fighting against poverty and human suffering offered a path to becoming a good and worthy person.

But such narratives became less compelling as the Great Depression and the war years gave way to improved economic conditions and opportunities. To my friends the narrative about the poor suffering Jew lost some of its power. We began to joke about the stereotypical image of the suffering Jew. We laughed as we sang the Yiddish song "Bulbes" (potatoes), a song that repeated the word "bulbes" when asked what the poor shtetel Jew ate each day of the week. A friend, Gene Bluestein, who became a professor of American culture, composed his own version of "Bulbes" called "Cheese And Cream" to jokingly mock Camp Kinderland's limited lunch menu. As Irving Howe observed, "There is nothing glamorous about poverty, nothing admirable about deprivation, nothing enviable about suffering. Whole areas of human possibilities and pleasures were blocked off."

My friend Gene Goodheart began his memoir about his Jewish experiences with the Yiddish lament "S'is schwer zu zein a Yid," (It's hard to be a Jew), not in the sense of Jewish suffering, but in knowing what it means to be Jewish. I've never had that problem. I've always knew what kind of Jew I was distinguishing myself from—religious Jews, Zionists, and non-Jewish Jews. The importance of marginal differences has been a common characteristic among religious and ethnic groups. But sustaining the thickness of my Jewish tradition in my own life, and passing it on to my children, has been difficult.

Here's the problem. As a child I learned Yiddish at home. For me as well as many of my friends, Yiddish was our first language. Yiddish provided the key that unlocked the door to my parents' lives in the Pale, and to their trials of immigration and their adjustment to American culture. Shuleh linked family to a larger Jewish community that connected me to something larger than myself. My Jewish identity expressed an important aspect of my individuality. That sense of difference mattered because it provided a space where I could recognize myself and feel at home. As I became more integrated into American culture, and my parents' world no longer played a central role in my daily life, it became more difficult to sustain that distinct Jewish tradition. Jewishness became less and less a part of who I was and how I lived. Yet I still trace many of my closest friends to those shared Jewish experiences.

I remember a moment that captures those continuing connections. In 1970, while a visiting professor at Yale University, I frequently spent time with Alan Trachtenberg, a member of the faculty and a close friend from Camp Lakeland, the adult resort connected to Camp Kinderland. One day I learned that my friend Herb Gutman, a distinguished historian and another former Kinderland camper, had been invited to lecture at Yale. I suggested that Trachtenberg and I meet him after his talk. I didn't know Herb as well as Alan and had not seen him for several years. But we greeted each other warmly and, after exchanging a few Yiddish expressions, old familiarities quickly unfolded.

I don't recall the conversation that night as we walked down the stairs of one of Yale's Tudor-style buildings. But I do remember stopping suddenly and, in a hushed voice, asking, "Do you think they'll find out?" They laughed knowingly. The question invited them to engage in old intimacies. But I was suggesting something more. While we had gained recognition from Yale, we were not yet fully accepted members of that venerable institution. Those tensions about our Jewish identity and the role it has played in our lives are reflected in Alan and Herb's work on American culture and on the role immigration and ethnicity have played in the lives of working people.

Sustaining a secular Jewish identity was hard enough, but shuleh added a complication. I was taught to be a Jew and a socialist, to identify with a particular cultural tradition while also valuing the ideals of human solidarity in the struggle for social justice. As I quickly discovered, maintaining my Jewish identity, and valuing universal ideals of solidarity and social justice, would not be easy. I learned this while walking through the ruins of my Bronx neighborhood with Leonid Gordon, a prominent Russian sociologist active in the reform movement that led to the collapse of the Soviet Union. He was part of a group of prominent Soviet social scientists and labor experts who participated in a conference I organized to evaluate Russia's transition from socialism to capitalism. I brought Leonid to the Bronx because I wanted him to see New York beyond the glitter and dazzle of Manhattan.

I had another agenda as well. Leonid had become a close friend with whom I wanted to share my childhood experiences. Walking through the streets of my old neighborhood, now predominantly Hispanic, I pointed to where my shuleh once stood and began describing my secular Jewish education. I was startled when he interrupted me and sharply asked, "What is all this Jewishness? I didn't think of you as someone preoccupied with such narrow parochial concerns."

Taken aback, I responded defensively, "But aren't you Jewish?"

"Yes," he replied, "but only by birth."

His warmth, his sense of humor, his skeptical disposition felt so Jewish to me. I remember a day in Moscow when he embraced me, exclaiming, "I can't explain it, but I feel that you have become a part of my family." I thought the intimacy he felt was an expression of our shared Jewish identity. What had I missed? I asked him about Soviet anti-Semitism, hoping it would trigger shared experiences. But he dismissed the problem as a minor aspect of Soviet repression and denied that anti-Semitism had affected the choices he had made in his life. It soon became clear that Leonid thought of himself, in Isaac Duetscher's words, as a "non-Jewish Jew."

The hostile way Leonid had responded to my Jewish identity troubled me. I wondered whether his accusation was a delayed response to a time in Moscow when Jack Sheinkman, President of the Amalgamated Clothing Workers' Union, had pulled me away from Leonid to meet a Russian Jew who had emigrated to Israel and had returned to Moscow to attend a conference on Jewish life in Russia. Leonid must have observed us standing on a crowded street conversing in Yiddish, our only shared language. He could not have known that most of the conversation was about the prevalence of Russian anti-Semitism.

Like many Marxists, Leonid believed that industrialization would create a more homogeneous working class. I asked him if he could explain the continuing need people had to identify with a particular culture or tradition. Didn't the persistence of religious and ethnic divisions pose some serious problems with Marx's predictions? He agreed that these were real problems, but he argued that technological change was gradually eliminating differences among groups, and that universal ideals of human solidarity would prevail over ethnic and national narrow-mindedness.

I'm not certain whether Leonid would have found any resonance in Isaiah Berlin's more personal defense of cultural identity and particularly Jewish identity. Berlin notes that "when men and women complain of loneliness, what they mean is that nobody understands what they are saying: to be understood is to share a common past, common feelings and language, intimate communications—in short to share common forms of life." Berlin believed that to be a Jew was to have a special understanding of this sense loneliness, and to know how profound the need is to belong. More than possessing land or statehood, belonging was a condition of being understood.

But is the need to belong compatible with my belief in socialist values? I shared Leonid's concern that identity politics have incubated social diseases tragically visible in ethnic and national conflicts. Yet ethnic and racial identity could also nurture feelings of empathy and compassion.

Separated from their homeland, my parents sought to create a new, meaningful life but one that sought to sustain their Jewish cultural traditions and to provide a place outside the dominant culture where they could be understood and "share common forms of life." Their search to belong was not only a strategy to cope with loneliness; it also nurtured feelings of compassion for others seeking a more just and meaningful life. Martin Luther King's struggle for social justice for African Americans was also a fight for greater political and economic rights for all people.

Leonid was mistaken. The 20th century cruelly revealed that ignoring the powerful need for belonging to a community is a recipe for disaster. Mass culture, consumerism, and impersonal markets that guide social and economic relations have broken down appearances of differences, yet as market relations have scoured away distinctiveness, people have become more defensive and assertive about what they believe are deeper connections and longings.

Chapter 2

THE SEARCH FOR BELONGING

FREUD CAPTURED THE POTENTIAL DANGERS of what he identified as the narcissism of minor differences. It is "precisely
the minor differences in people who are otherwise alike that
form the basis of feelings of strangeness and hostility between
them." Yet for many, those differences provide a space where they
can be understood. If Isaiah Berlin is correct, those "shared forms
of life" are not minor but are for many an existential human need.

My childhood experiences provide no clear answer to the questions Leonid raised and continue to trouble my utopian dreams.
As I was walking innocently down a street a few blocks from my
apartment three older boys stepped out from behind a building and
blocked my path. "Hey, kid," one menacingly asked, "are you Jewish?"

How does a ten-year-old boy respond to such a threat? "No,"

I said, hoping that they would let me pass.

But just as these Italian boys could not hide their identity, I could not hide mine. They laughed and one of the boys shouted, "Drop your pants and prove it." Reacting instinctively, I turned and ran as fast as I could until I reached the safety of my block. I had many other similar encounters. Life on the streets had taught me that being Jewish could be dangerous.

The violence and aggression that is used to sustain loyalty to a group is not only directed outward but also inward to suppress differences that threaten group loyalty. Only half awake, Alice picked up the phone that rang at two in the morning. Suddenly I heard her shout, "Who are you?" Slamming down the phone she turned to me and said, "Someone just threatened to rape and kill me."

The phone rang again. I picked it up. A menacing voice shouted, "We know who you are, where you teach, and where you live. We know all about Jews like you who collaborate with our enemies to destroy Israel. Your days are numbered."

Attempting to learn more about the caller, I responded, "We're not anti-Israel." I began speaking in Yiddish, hoping it would create some common ground. But he cut me off shouting, "Don't use that gutter language with me." Svetlana Boym has elegantly written, "The moment we try to repair longing with belonging, the apprehension of loss with the discovery of identity, we often part ways and put an end to mutual understanding."

I am married to a respected feminist historian with whom I have worked on many projects. We share the same goal of diminishing barriers and divisions that undermine efforts to create a just and democratic society. Many of Alice's feminist colleagues are a part of our circle of friends. I thought of myself as a member of this community. And so, when Gerda Lerner, a leading historian of women, announced to a small group of friends, who had gathered in the apartment of the peace activist and feminist Amy Swerdlow, that she had some important business to discuss, I anticipated participating in an interesting conversation.

But Gerda had no intention of including the two men in the room. I could not tell what Amy's husband Stanley was feeling when Gerda announced that the women retreat to another room so that they could have a serious conversation. Stanley, who was suffering from advanced Parkinson's disease, just stared blankly ahead. Stunned, I looked at him and said, "We've just been relegated to the kitchen."

In my utopian dreams I imagined ways of reducing the social divisions that divided identity groups by appealing to shared ideals of social justice and democratic participation. Is the rise of identity politics inimical to those aspirations? At a time when group loyalty is becoming more difficult to sustain, many still believe that belonging to a particular group is permanent and unchanging. Yet countless others also share a desire to be a part of something bigger than any one group. Such feelings can be used to unite people from diverse backgrounds. But when attachment to a particular group fosters a politics based on difference, it creates walls that divide us and weaken movements for social reform.

I learned to pay particular attention to the special role that racism played in dividing Americans. My upbringing led me to be mindful of racism in its open and more hidden manifestations. When the word describing people of color changed from Negro to

Black and then to African American, I accepted the argument that words matter in the fight for racial justice. As I marched with my White and Black friends shouting, "Blacks and Whites together, we shall not be moved," I felt a part of a larger struggle to overcome divisions that stood in the way of progressive social change. But experience has taught me how difficult it is to overcome ethnic and racial animosities.

When Tolstoy wrote, "God is the name of my desire," did he mean that most of us need some transcendent belief in the face of the inevitability of illness, old age, loneliness, and death? In a letter to Freud, Romaine Rolland suggests that religious belief originated in feelings of something limitless and unbounded. He used the term "oceanic" to describe a sense of being one with the universe. These feelings, he argued, are not based on religious faith or a belief in immortality. They exist for many people, even for those who accept Freud's argument that religion is an illusion. Was this what Mom meant when she said that we are all a part of nature? Was this the source of my utopian disposition? Freud would have none of this. For him the oceanic feeling was another way the developing ego deflected the dangers it faced from the external world.

The need to be loved and to connect with others is an essential human trait. It is revealed when we express compassion and sympathy for strangers. But how deep and wide is human empathy? It is Freud who warns us that the commandment "to love your neighbor as yourself" is an untenable ethical goal. Faced with evidence of unspeakable human cruelty, Freud proclaimed that it was time to give up our youthful illusions about the healing power of love.

I first encountered Freud's anti-utopian message in an under-graduate course taught by Professor Axelrod, a distinguished psy-choanalyst. Not long into the semester I began to challenge Freud's pessimistic assessment of human nature. Still, I was attracted to Freud's search for the hidden sources of human behavior and neu-rosis. As a budding Marxist I had a different view of the human capacity for good and evil. I accepted Freud's view that ethical commandments could not by themselves end violence and cruelty. But I countered that, if we change the social and economic con-ditions that breed violence, we can learn to live more cooperatively and peacefully. I agreed that by itself love would not end violence and cruelty. Without justice love remained an empty slogan. As Martin Luther King would soon preach: "Justice is love correcting that which revolts against love."

During our discussions, Professor Axelrod would frequently turn to me and ask, "So what does the sociologist think?" I believe he meant socialist, but this was the height of the McCarthy hysteria, and he didn't want to stigmatize me. I sensed he liked me. On the last day of class, he pulled me aside and in a soft, caring voice warned, "Be careful, Bert. Don't put all your eggs in one basket."

I walked away uncertain about the meaning of his message. Was this about the threat posed by McCarthy, or was it something more personal? I knew my political interests were different from most of my classmates'. I felt out of step with the growing con-sumer culture and the turn from civic to private concerns. The America of my childhood was rapidly changing.

My political convictions were formed during the Second World War, when the Communist Party was proclaiming a new Americanism. It was a moment when the Soviet Union and United States were allies, and communists were promoting a popular front to unite all Americans in the fight against fascism. Paul Robeson's rendition of "The Ballad for America," and Frank Sinatra singing the "The House I Live In," symbolized what a united America might be like. I still remember Paul Robeson's deep resounding voice proclaiming, "From the plains and the mountains we have sprung, to keep the faith with those who went before."

Those efforts to promote ethnic and racial diversity infused my youthful idealism. I participated in a leadership program organized by the IWO, where I was taught to distinguish between chauvinism and ethnic pride, and between national superiority and patriotism. The message was clear: We should be proud of our ethnic heritage but reject efforts to use our differences to undermine our shared values. It was a time of war when I felt a deep bond to America's ideals. I listed General Dwight Eisenhower as my hero in my elementary school album. I listened to folk music and jazz and read novels by John Steinbeck and Howard Fast. I cried when Ma Joad exclaimed, "Can't nobody lick us. We'll go on forever. We're the people."

I recall the excitement I felt as I prepared to dance on the stage of Carnegie Hall at an event celebrating Soviet– American friendship. I was twelve, anxiously waiting to play my part in a dance commemorating the Soviet Union's battle against German fascism. Suddenly Edith Segal, my dance teacher, grabbed my hand and pulled me toward someone who had just come backstage. "This is Paul Robeson," she said. "He will be performing with you."

I looked up in awe at this very tall man. Smiling, he bent down, lifted me into the air, and hugged me. From that moment I associated Robeson's rich base voice with those powerful hands and his warm embrace. I would see him once again, in 1949, at a concert he was giving in Peekskill, New York, that would end in violence. I admired him then. Only later did I become troubled when I discovered his failure to expose Stalin's purges and the execution of Jewish writers.

I said that my formal education in utopia began in shuleh. That's not quite accurate. Shuleh introduced me to two versions of utopia, one romantic and cultural, and the other scientific and knowing. They blended almost seamlessly into my education about the coming of a new society. As we moved from elementary to more advanced courses, the study of Jewish culture and history was examined through the lens of Marxist theories of society and economy. In the beginning I hardly noticed the difference. Both cultural and economic interpretations spoke about problems of poverty and exploitation and a future of hope and deliverance.

As my education unfolded, the more romantic visions of socialism faded. I learned to distinguish between utopian dreams and scientific laws of history. I remember laughing at my friend Ray for sobbing while watching the film *National Velvet*. "What relevance does a film about horses and rural life have for a poor Jewish Bronx boy?" When he responded that he hoped that someday he could live on a farm with horses, I laughed and called him a silly dreamer. And yet I secretly shared his fantasies.

I would never openly admit such thoughts to my Marxist friends who, like me, were beginning to learn about the laws of history. History, we were taught, could only be grasped by understanding the social and economic forces that determined its direction. We learned that socialism emerges from the failures of capitalism. Socialism was not some idealized society to which reality would have to adjust but rather develops as part of the struggles of workers against an unjust and crisis-ridden social order. Like the Christian belief in transcendence and redemption, I was taught that the only authentic vision of the future depended on the failure of the present.

I wondered when this would happen. The Russian Revolution and the recent Chinese Revolution had revealed that life beyond capitalism already existed for most people. I learned that unlocking the secrets of capitalist development was not an easy task. Only hardheaded economic and historical analysis could reveal the direction of capitalist development and the promise of a new society.

At the age of eighteen I could recite by rote the hidden source of capitalist profits and of workers' exploitation. To the question: What determines the value of a commodity? I would respond, "The value of a commodity is determined by the socially necessary labor time embodied in its production." And when asked, What is the value of the social necessary labor used in the production of a commodity? I'd reply, "The value of the socially necessary labor used in production is the customary cost of living necessary to support the worker's capacity to work and raise a family." Then came the key question. And what is surplus value? I would proudly say, "Surplus value is the source of capitalist profits, the hidden secret of worker's exploitation. It is the difference between the value of commodities created by workers and what the bosses pay the workers to live." With a knowing smile I would say, "The wealth of our society is built on the exploitation of workers."

Marxist dialectics held a special attraction. It made me feel a part of something important that gave purpose and meaning to my life. I began to see my father in a different light. I saw his working-class credentials as a badge of honor rather than derision. I read with pride Marx's words that the insurgent proletariat represents "in the midst of degradation, the revolt against degradation" and a vision of a new society. "What the bourgeoisie. . .produces above all are its gravediggers. Its fall, and the victory of the proletariat, are equally inevitable."

I repeated my father's stories about his work in Harlem and the black celebrities he met. I recounted how his store was spared during the Harlem riots of 1939 because his customers and fellow workers respected him. I embellished tales of how he helped unionize his store and how the union had helped make life better for us. I began to resist my mother's criticism of his lack of ambition. In her eyes my father was someone I should not emulate. While she supported the worker's struggle for a better life, she wanted me to escape the hardships of working-class life. Today,, when progressive friends gather in an expensive restaurant I often teasingly say, "There's nothing too good for the working class."

Like a Talmudic scholar, I looked to Marxist texts for answers to the question: How will capitalism end? Marx's obstetric historical theory suggested that the birth of socialism could only come when workers believed that capitalism did not work. For this to happen, things needed to get bad before they got better. This worldview put me in a rather peculiar position. While I hoped for a better world, I also eagerly looked for signs of capitalist decay and crisis. I did not openly admit it, but I believed that the worst of times would be followed by the best of times. The Great Depression and the war against fascism had confirmed those feelings. I looked back at this terrible moment in history as a time of great promise and confirmation of the forward march of history. It was a point in my life when I felt intimately connected to America.

The onset of the Second World War enhanced my boyhood fantasies about the coming of a new world order. The heroic battles of Stalingrad and Leningrad affirmed my faith in socialism. I sang Yiddish and Russian songs honoring the heroism of the Soviet people's resistance against German fascism. I sang, "Fly higher and higher and higher, our emblem is the Soviet star, and every propeller is singing red front defending the USSR." I thought I knew something my classmates did not: The fight against fascism was only the beginning of an unfolding historical movement toward socialism.

But I had other pressing things on my mind. Sex had entered the lives of my friends, and I felt left out. They seemed to know something I did not. I listened in silence to their stories of wet dreams and sexual fantasies, nodding as if I too shared those experiences. More and more of our conversations turned to girls and male bravado. I felt dishonest and ashamed. I didn't want them to discover that I had not yet experienced the celebrated moment of ejaculation. I did not understand at the time that politics and sex were intimately linked.

These feelings of humiliation had been with me for a while. At the age of thirteen I noticed that my twin sister's body began to change. She began to assume the shape of a young woman. She stood three inches taller than me and looked like my older sister.

We still shared a room in our small apartment, with little opportunity for privacy. Differences in our sexual development led to tensions and conflict. I dreaded visits to family and friends and the inevitable biting words, "Look how much taller she is." The usual assurances that boys develop later than girls didn't help.

By the age of fifteen nature unlocked its unkindly grip. Now much taller than my sister and more fully matured, I participated more freely and honestly in our sexual fantasies and adventures. I remember the excitement in Ray's voice when he yelled from the street below my apartment window, "Come down! I have something special to tell you." He had just returned from a summer job in Camp Kinderland. I ran down the five flights of stairs, and as soon as I opened the door, he shouted, "I got laid!"

I was stunned. "Tell me everything." I knew as I clung to his every word that Ray had crossed a big divide that separated boyish fantasies from real experiences.

So I was taken aback when, a few months later, the director of the Hecher Cursen (Higher Courses) suggested that I lead a discussion on sexuality and women's rights. He informed me that a student had made inappropriate sexual remarks to one of the younger female teachers, and that such behavior could not be tolerated in our school. He then told me that as president of the student body I needed to raise greater awareness about this problem with the student body. I had my marching orders. I called for a special meeting to discuss what was then called "The Woman Question."

I wasn't sure how to proceed. We were teenage boys, and sexual desire had assumed an important role in our relations with girls. How does a boy in the early stages of sexual discovery lead a political conversation on "the woman question"? Did my sexual desires conflict with values of gender equality? I felt unqualified to lead such a discussion. But as President of Club Freedman, I felt it was my duty to do it. And so, I turned to one of the older boys who I thought knew more about the subject. I asked Sol Jolty for help.

Sol would later host a popular WBAI radio program on car repair. He would also become known for an article he wrote, during the sexual revolution in the late 1960s, calling for a movement in defense of asexuality. I approached the young Jolty while he was holding court in the lounge area of the school. He was an imposing figure—tall, with a large humped back and a deep base voice. With some trepidation I told him what had happened and asked him how he thought I should conduct the meeting. He responded, in a loud booming voice that everyone could hear, "Have you read Lenin on the women question?"

"No," I answered, embarrassed by my apparent ignorance.

"Read it," he said. "That's all you will need to know to conduct the meeting." And so I began to organize the assembly without consulting any of the girls in our class.

What a disaster. Standing before the assembly, I suggested that sex was the source of women's oppression, and if we really believed in equality between men and women, the boys needed to show more control over their sexual feelings and treat women with respect. Citing Lenin, I concluded that unfettered sex was like drinking from a dirty glass of water.

There was a deafening silence. No one spoke. Some of the boys began to laugh. Finally, one of our teachers got up and said, "This

is not about sex. It is about treating all our teachers with respect."
The meeting ended with a suggestion that the accused student write
a letter of apology to the female faculty member.

Hope is an essential ingredient for those who dream of new
ways of living. Such sentiments are nurtured when large numbers
of people reach out beyond their private interests and seek to improve the social and economic conditions of their lives. But as the
economist Albert Hirschman noted, such periods of civic engagement are difficult to sustain. I remember the jubilation in my neighborhood when the war ended, and block parties marked the onset
of more normal times. It did not take too long before I noticed the
difference.

The world of my youth rapidly changed. In the late 1940s the
Soviet Union, once an ally, became an enemy and a threat to our
national security. The fight against communism replaced the war
against fascism and what it meant to be an American. It seemed as
if everything had just been turned upside down. As I marched
down 10th Avenue in Manhattan's Hell's Kitchen in 1947, celebrating May Day, I noticed a large group of people standing on the
sidewalk, gesturing and yelling at passing marchers. At first, I
thought they were workers expressing their support; after all, Hell's
Kitchen was a working-class neighborhood.

I was mistaken. Suddenly, a large group of those workers
started running toward us, carrying sticks and yelling, "Go back
to Russia, you commie bastards!" I looked around for help, hoping
that veterans participating in the march would protect us. But they
weren't there. I had recently fractured my wrist and my left arm
was protected by a large plastic cast. My friend Ray and I turned

and ran to escape a mob of older boys racing toward us. I was too slow. I felt a stick strike the cast and I stumbled to the ground. When I looked up, I saw them running in the opposite direction, with the police in pursuit. I felt a sense of relief but utter bewilderment. I had just been attacked by workers and saved by the police. This was not how the world was supposed to work.

I was no longer in sync with America. The promise of a grand coalition in pursuit of equality and democracy was quickly fading. For a boy of sixteen, this shifting reality was confusing. I struggled to understand what was happening. U.S.– Soviet cooperation had ended. Anti-communism began to dominate American politics. My values had not changed, but a new political culture was challenging some of my core beliefs. My efforts to make sense of these rapidly changing circumstances were made more difficult because the community of which I was a part resisted altering its beliefs in the face of contradictory evidence.

There was another complication. As I moved from childhood to adolescence, I encountered, not one, but two utopian visions that competed for my attention. The first was more ubiquitous. It fostered utopian ideals of unbounded promises of American capitalism. Let us call it the fantasies of the Lone Ranger, a utopian idea that sought to inspire dreams of social mobility and a life of freedom and independence. It also nourished Oedipal fantasies of lifting one's parents out of their meager social and economic existence. Few could fully escape its hold on our aspirations and imagination.

This utopian vision turned the self-made man (not woman) into a heroic figure who rises above all hurdles to create a better world. During the war years such stories of heroism were everywhere.

They would soon become part of the neo-liberal imagination. The enemies of this utopian vision were the government regulations and social institutions that limited our freedom to choose and restricted the creative power of a free market. Trade unions and, in some versions, even acts of kindness were targeted as enemies of freedom. Many years later I discovered the importance that the neo-liberal economist Friedrich Hayek placed on promoting the idea of a liberal utopia. As he exclaimed the year after the Second World War ended:

> We must make the building of a free society once more an intellectual adventure, a deed of courage. What we lack is a liberal Utopia. . .a truly radical liberalism. . .the main lesson which the true liberal must learn from the success of the socialists is that it was their courage to be Utopian which gained them the support of the intellectuals.

The sensibilities embedded Hayek's utopia continue to play a significant role in American culture. Its vision is nurtured by the relentless struggle to achieve wealth and status. No wonder so many respond nostalgically and sympathetically to Frank Sinatra singing "I Did It My Way." While I was not completely immune to the song's allure, I was nurtured by a different vision, one dependent on feelings of fairness and social justice and on ways working and living more cooperatively.

Shuleh and family provided the initial inspiration for such sentiments. Camp Lakeland provided the setting and environment where my utopian ideals could fully flourish. Set in a wooded area surrounded by a beautiful lake, Camp Lakeland provided a refuge for mostly Jewish workers attached to the Jewish Peoples Fraternal Order (JPFO) and for parents visiting their children in Camp Kinderland. Unlike many of my friends, I did not have the Kinderland experience. But I did experience working at Camp Lakeland. In 1948 at the age of seventeen, Lakeland provided the setting where my utopian disposition blossomed. For three long summers from the age of seventeen to nineteen, fueled by Eros and hormones, I began to feel a sense of empowerment. Freed from family responsibilities and nurtured by a community that shared many of my values and beliefs, I began a relationship that would profoundly change my life.

Camp Kinderland and its adult counterpart, Camp Lakeland, were a part of a larger effort to promote the ideology and educational philosophy of the shuleh movement. The Workman's Circle, the social democratic competitor of the JPFO, built its children's camp (Kinder Ring) directly across Sylvan Lake. Both camps shared goals of promoting Yiddishkeit and a commitment to social and economic justice. But because of their anti-Soviet views, we thought of the Workman's Circle as enemies, labeling them "social fascists"—a term leveled by communists in Germany in the early 1930s against socialists they thought were collaborating with fascists. Once again, I was forced to make distinctions that I did not fully understand. In those days the Soviet Union loomed as a leader in the heroic struggle against fascism and a beacon in the struggle for a socialist future.

Camp Lakeland was more than an extension of my shuleh experiences. The intensity and intimacy of our work and living conditions cemented friendships that would last a lifetime. We were beneficiaries of a generation born in the 1920s who had experienced the Great Depression and the Second World War, and who were drawn into the great debates about building a socialist future. We took Marx at his word. We could change the direction of history. And while we were deeply troubled by how the Cold War had transformed domestic politics, we were encouraged that more and more of the world's population had embraced socialism.

But such worldly problems were a small part of our daily concerns. For many of us Lakeland provided a rite of passage from adolescence to adulthood, a quest for intimacy and love, and a different way of living and wanting. The term "comrade" comes to mind as I reflect on those times. I have used the word when asked to speak at the funerals of departed friends to convey the special quality of friendships based on bonds of shared values and experiences that enriched our lives and the lives of others.

We bonded around the pranks and games we played with their not-so-subtle sexual undercurrents. I remember an incident when we almost lost our jobs. One night at a gathering in one of the bunks in the Bowery, a plan was hatched to doing something playfully provocative to the female counselors. We had heard of other raids that had taken place in the past, but our intention was to do something outrageous. Armed with a dozen eggs taken from the kitchen, we silently enter a bunk where a female counselor slept. At a designated time, each of us cracked open an egg on the face of a sleeping counselor. I heard their screams as we ran back to the Bowery. The raid was the talk of the camp. The girls were angry but also playful in their response, threating retaliation. We hoped that would happen.

Management was not so forgiving. An emergency meeting was hastily called. We were told that what had happened was nothing short of an attack on the camp. Chaver Cohen, the camp director, demanded that we reveal the names of those who participated in such shameful behavior. Our first response was laughter and then silence. Did he really believe that we would betray a fellow worker? He then began to question our loyalty to the camp. Those responsible had not only wasted a dozen eggs but had placed an unnecessary burden on those working in the laundry.

The camp director's concern for the workers rang hollow. We called our living quarters the Bowery, named after a place in Manhattan known for its squalid rooming houses reserved for the most down-and-out of the working class. Partly an attempt at humor but also a not-so-veiled criticism of our living conditions, the Bowery's cabins made privacy virtually impossible. Each cabin was divided into four small rooms containing two beds but no closet. The walls separating the units were made of thin wooden panels, often pock-marked with cracks and holes. There were no windows only screens that provided little protection from the weather. Clothes and towels were hung on nails or placed in suitcases under our beds. Toilets and showers were housed in a small building on a hill above the living quarters, its distance from our cabins painfully revealed one night when almost everybody in Bowery was inflicted with diarrhea.

If the managers of the camp were so concerned about the workers in the laundry, why didn't they do something to improve our living conditions? Shouldn't workers in a progressive camp have a role to play in how the camp was managed? Summer was coming to an end, but we had begun to question whether our shared values were consistent with camp practices. We decided to organize a workers committee to confront management's proclaimed belief in workers' rights.

The following summer, as the chairman of the workers committee, I was asked to meet with Chaver Cohen. The meeting was hastily arranged after we threatened to call a strike if our demands for improved living conditions were not met. We assembled in Chaver Cohen's bungalow, a modest house consisting of a small kitchen, a bathroom, a living room and three bedrooms. Yet it seemed palatial compared to our small, modest cabins. As I looked around, I wondered why the leaders of a socialist camp tolerated such disparities.

Cohen began the meeting by berating me for threatening to strike against a socialist camp committed to serving workers and their children. "Why do you want to damage the reputation of our camp? Rather than threatening to strike, it was your responsibility to foster cooperation, not conflict, between workers and managers."

Taken aback I responded defensively. "But look how you live and how we live. How could you justify such differences?" He dismissed my criticism by arguing that the house had been built, not only for the camp director, but also as a place where important visitors could stay.

I knew that the kitchen workers would not support a strike, and conversations with friends indicated that there was little enthusiasm for an act that might threaten their jobs and income. Nor did we want to damage the camp's reputation. So I accepted assurances that management would do more to improve our living conditions. Still, I was troubled by Chaver Cohen's unwillingness to acknowledge the inconsistency between his professed socialist values and our working conditions, which did not significantly change during the years I worked in Camp Lakeland.

Our rudimentary living conditions were compensated for by the freedom we enjoyed and our rich social and cultural life. After work we gathered at the casino, a building where I participated in dance, choral, and theater productions. While occasionally more distinguished guest artists or lecturers were invited, the counselors and the dining room staff provided the talent for the shows. It was also the space where more intimate relations were formed.

As soon as Edith Segal spotted me one night walking toward the casino, I knew my fate was sealed. When we were younger, my sister and I had participated in a dance group she directed that would occasionally perform at trade union meetings. Edith gave me a big hug and announced, "I have a special part for you in my next production." I hesitated. I wasn't sure I wanted to spend my free time this way. But before I could respond she exclaimed, "You must see this as your political responsibility as a worker in this camp." So once again I became a part of Edith's lifelong passion to use dance as a political weapon.

Dancing for Edith had less lofty and more personal consequences. I met Evelyn while performing in Edith's dance group. I thought I had found someone with whom I could share my hopes and dreams. Evelyn introduced me to her welcoming family, who deepened my network of friends. Our relationship began at the end of the summer of 1949. It was a moment when my personal and social lives were tightly bound.

But it soon became evident that Evelyn was struggling with difficult psychological challenges. Despite her warmth she often retreated into private reflections, unable to talk about the despondency she was feeling. At times when we were alone, she would suddenly and without warning begin to cry. When I pleaded with her to tell me what was wrong, she would only say, "I don't know, I don't know." After much prodding she spoke about her mother who had recently died, and her father's plan to remarry. I assumed those deeply unsettling events in her life were the causes of her melancholy, and I encouraged her to talk about her feelings of loss and abandonment. But the more I probed, the more she withdrew into herself. When the summer ended, I thought our approaching separation was fortuitous. I was about to begin college uncertain about what I wanted to study and how best to manage the competing demands of college and political activism. Evelyn lived in Brooklyn and decided to attend Brooklyn College. I chose Queens College, partly because I thought the separation would give me more time to pursue my own interests.

It did not work exactly as planned. Evelyn wanted more of my time. But travelling to Brooklyn each weekend interfered with studying and my other obligations. While I could manage the demands of the humanities courses, I could not depend solely on my lecture notes in chemistry and physics. The highly motivated, mostly Jewish pre-med students had organized study groups I could not attend to help them prepare for weekly exams. By the end of the first semester, I realized that I could not be politically active, study science, and see Evelyn. I decided to change my major from biochemistry to sociology and economics. I also began to question my relationship with Evelyn.

Was I missing something? Were my expectations misplaced? Evelyn seemed more withdrawn and distant. It became more difficult to share my apprehensions and aspirations with her. One night when we were alone, I told her that I wanted to end the relationship and hoped we could still be friends. She just nodded and said nothing. I felt I had done something terrible. She seemed so sad. I worried about what she might do or say.

The responses of my friends surprised me. The following evening a group of friends, including Evelyn's sister and brother-in-law, came to see me. They told me I had made a terrible mistake. Evelyn was miserable. Why was I doing this to her? Didn't I care about her? I didn't know how to respond. Was there a hidden threat in their efforts to bring us back together? Had I broken an expected code of conduct? I relented, and we resumed our relationship. I did not foresee what would happen four months later.

One cold Saturday evening in November 1950, Evelyn's father asked if he could speak to me. "Sure," I said. "Is Evelyn okay?"

"Well, that's what I wanted to talk to you about. I think she's depressed."

"Yes." I nodded. "I've been worrying about that, too." Before I could say anything else, he grabbed my hand and said, "I know why she is so sad, and I think you can do something about it. I'm not an educated man, and I'm not a psychologist, but I know my daughter. She's unhappy because she misses you and wants to be with you. If you love her, there is an easy solution. You should marry my daughter."

Stunned, I exclaimed, "That's impossible. How can we get married? We need to finish college. We can't afford to get married."

I thought that would end the conversation. Evelyn then entered the room. She seemed embarrassed but clearly knew what her father was proposing. I repeated what I had said, thinking she would agree. But to my surprise she said. "I think it could work. I'll leave college and find a job."

I told her that would be a mistake.

Her father then said, "Do you want to marry my daughter?" Evelyn seemed embarrassed.

Confused, I blurted out, "Yes, but not now."

Her father would not accept my answer. He tried a different tactic. "This may be the best time for you to marry. It would keep you out of the army." It was the time of the Korean War, and young men my age were being inducted into military service. I told him they were not drafting students.

But he insisted that would change. "By marrying you could avoid ever serving. And nothing will change." He looked at his daughter and me and said, "I have a plan that will solve everything. You'll marry and not *be* married."

I was still confused.

"Look," he said, "getting married is just a formality. It's a piece of paper that you sign. You sign this paper, but you live separately. Only the immediate family needs to know. And you no longer need worry about the draft."

I was speechless.

He looked at me and again asked, "Don't you want to marry my daughter?"

I didn't know how to respond. I remember looking at Evelyn and her father and saying, "Okay, that might work. I need to talk to my parents."

Mom looked at me in disbelief. "You're not *serious*? You're too young to get married. You need to finish school." My father started to laugh. That was a mistake.

I looked at them and shouted, "I'm not child, and I'm doing this." The following day I approached my mother and said, "Look, I'm not *really* getting married. I'll still be living at home. Isn't this a good way of staying out of the army?"

She sighed and reluctantly said, "Okay, but I think you're making a mistake."

We were married on a dreary December day in 1950 in the basement of a house owned by a friend of Evelyn's family. I was nineteen years old. Only my parents, my sister, Evelyn's father, her sisters, and his new wife were invited.

Since Evelyn's father was not a believer, I was surprised that he had asked a rabbi to conduct the ceremony. But it was brief, and after a few pleasantries, we left. I thought life would return to the way it had been. In fact, it did. I continued my studies and saw Evelyn and friends on weekends. No one suspected that we were married.

Can you be married and not be married? Yes, such arrangements are common among immigrants seeking entry into the United States. But Evelyn could not sustain the façade. She complained about living in close quarters with her father's new extended family.

In May she told me that she no longer wanted to live apart. She planned to take a leave of absence from college so that we could afford to get married.

I resisted, to no avail. Evelyn's father began to plan a June wedding.

George Bernard Shaw's well-known quip that youth is wasted on the young seems so knowing when looking back on our youthful follies and dreams. "If only I knew then what I know now" is the common refrain. Yet I have no regrets. What wisdom I have acquired has been enriched by my youthful mistakes. My mother's refrain that experience is the best teacher provides a necessary corrective to Shaw's facile comment. My values matured by challenging my most deeply held beliefs. When the sociologist Daniel Bell was asked to reflect on his early socialist and Marxist views, he responded somewhat dismissively, "What did we know, we were so young?" Yet those youthful experiences contributed to his intellectual development and achievements.

Chapter 3

THE END OF COMMUNISM

O N AUGUST 28, 1949, ON MY EIGHTEENTH birthday I joined the Communist Party. It was an act of defiance, a response to disturbing events that had occurred the previous evening. On the afternoon of August 27, many Kinderland and Lakeland staff decided to attend a Paul Robeson concert in Peekskill, New York. For security reasons some staff were asked to remain behind.

Late that evening our friends returned with disturbing news. A mob of enraged men supported by the Veterans of Foreign Wars and the American Legion had tried to block their entry to the concert grounds. They managed to find another way to get through the barriers and reached the stage, where a few hundred people had gathered. They were warned that an angry mob had assembled and was preparing to attack them. Following the novelist Howard

Fast's direction, they began organizing a defense against what they thought was an imminent assault. Men had begun forming a circle around the women and children when suddenly the lights went out. Everyone ran to their cars and buses. As they drove out of the campground, they were met by an angry rock-throwing mob, injuring some people.

A sense of impending danger spread through the camp. We were told of a possible assault because a regional newspaper had published a map exposing the location of all the left-leaning camps in Northern Westchester County. An emergency meeting was called. Staff was asked to defend the campground against possible intruders. Holding a baseball bat while standing guard into the early morning hours, I felt deeply disturbed by the dangerously shifting political climate.

The next afternoon I was invited to a special meeting on the grounds of the tennis courts located near our living quarters. When I arrived, approximately fifty counselors and Lakeland staff had already assembled. Pete Seeger began singing. Speakers spoke of Peekskill as a harbinger of ominous political times and the importance of mobilizing people in defense our freedom. As the meeting ended, Seeger began strumming his banjo, encouraging people to join the Communist Party.

Al pulled Ray and me aside and asked if we could talk. He was a few years our senior. Muscular but soft-spoken, he had served in the army during the war. We walked to my bunk in the Bowery and sat on my bed.

He began speaking about Peekskill and the importance of organizing against the emerging threat of fascism. He stressed the

Communist Party's special role in the resistance and invited us to join, acknowledging the dangers that came with party membership. Communists were being closely watched and persecuted. Many of the Party leaders were facing imprisonment under the Smith Act. To protect us from possible reprisals no official documentation of our membership would be kept. He paused and waited for our response. Ray and I looked at each other and nodded. Al shook our hands and had us sign membership cards. He then tore the cards into small pieces and pushed them through cracks in the floorboards.

Despite possible threats of violence, I learned that a second concert had been scheduled for September 4. This time I joined thousands to hear Robeson, Seeger, and others perform. Hundreds of union members, veterans, and volunteers formed a circle around the stage to protect the performers against an attack. The concert went off without a hitch. But the concert did not end peacefully. A mob had assembled as we exited the grounds. I saw police standing idly by as rocks were thrown at buses and cars. My friends and I escaped without injury, but many others were hurt. I had a sinking feeling that the America of my childhood had ended. My simple hopes were gone.

My membership in the Communist Party lasted less than a year. On a Saturday afternoon in October 1949, I attended my first meeting. To protect the security of Party members, I knew only the identity of those in my unit. Our group of ten met in the Bronx apartment of one of the members.

After a few months I began to wonder whether I had made a mistake. At each meeting we were given material outlining the

Party's position on a particular political issue. At first, I thought the meetings would provide opportunities for discussion and deliberation, and our ideas would be shared with the leadership. That's not what happened. Each month a representative from the Party turned up, not to discuss what we had read, but rather whether we understood its content and how it should be used. I quickly learned that posing too many questions raised doubts about my Party discipline. I found the meetings boring and unproductive and began avoiding them. It was the beginning of my disenchantment with the Communist Party. By the end of the year, I no longer attended meetings and finally decided to end my membership in the Party.

On August 28, 1949, the night I joined the Party, I had believed I had crossed an important milestone in my life. Lying on a blanket near a raging fire, I'd felt deep connection to a community that embodied so many of my hopes and dreams. Those sentiments were suddenly disrupted when I heard the words "You've got a birthday, we have none, we sing to you," ring out as everyone joined in singing the camp's birthday song and chanting. "Speech, speech!" Overwhelmed, I was unable to express what I felt at that moment. So I simply thanked everyone for being an important part of my life.

As the night faded and we drifted into silent reflection someone jumped to his feet and shouted, "Okay, girls, it's time for you to leave. Boys, get ready to put out the fire." There was laughter as the girls moved into the shadows and we gathered around the diminishing flames, ready to perform a traditional ritual. The sound of urine splashing on the fire brought more laughter as some of boys began crowing about the power and distance of their flowing streams. Many years later I discovered a footnote in *Civilization and Its Discontents*, Freud's analysis of a deeper meaning to our gendered ritual:

> It is as though primal man had the habit, when he came in contact with fire, of satisfying an infantile desire to connect with it, by putting it out with the stream of his urine. . .a theme to which modern giants, Gulliver in Lilliput and Rabelais' Gargantua, still hark back—was therefore, a kind of sexual act with a male, an enjoyment of sexual potency in a homosexual competition. It was as though women had been appointed guardian of the fire, which was held captive on the domestic hearth, because her anatomy made it impossible for her to yield to the temptation of this desire.

Were my early perceptions of an ideal community connected to male bonding? Many of my experiences in Camp Lakeland were gendered. Alliances with names like The Yakels and Eight Balls were formed to foster special friendships and loyalties among the boys. They were our special version of a college fraternity.

Those distinctive bonds would soon be tested. In October 1949, after a ten-month trial, the top leaders of the Communist Party were convicted under the Smith Act for conspiring to overthrow the government of the United States. The press and public opinion supported the verdict. Outside events were used to promote a mounting fear of communism. The Soviet Union had exploded an atomic bomb, communists had prevailed in the Chinese

Civil War, and the House Un-American Activities Committee began its search for communists and their sympathizers.

I first encountered McCarthyism at Queens College. Herb Gutman, who had recently graduated, encouraged me to go. I remember his booming voice: "Great teachers, small classes, be sure to take a course with Vera Shlakman. You won't be sorry." I did enroll in Vera Shlakman's labor economics course but not until the fall of 1952, at a time when faculty were subpoenaed to appear before the Un-American Activities Committee. I don't remember exactly how many classes I attended before Professor Shlakman was asked to testify. Was I imagining the tension in her voice as I listened to her last lecture? I do remember how stunned I was when a young instructor walked into our classroom and announced that he would be our new teacher.

Leo Kaplan began the class by conceding that we had lost a wonderful professor and, to my surprise, announced he would give us an opportunity to discuss what had happened. He then left, saying he would return in fifteen minutes. Stunned and troubled, I remember angrily suggesting we find ways of voicing our opposition to her dismissal. While other students spoke in support of some action, most seemed confused and conflicted, insisting we did not have enough information to take any action. When Leo Kaplan returned, he assured us he would try to teach the course Professor Shlakman planned to offer.

What he said disarmed me. Some years later I told him that his comments probably undermined my efforts to organize resistance to Professor Shlakman's dismissal. But I doubt much could have been done. An atmosphere of fear and apprehension had taken root among the faculty. No significant protests surfaced in support of those who had lost their jobs during that period of political repression.

A friend, the political scientist Martin Fleischer, recalled an incident that captures the anxiety and wariness that infected universities. In 1954 he had circulated a petition among Columbia University faculty protesting violations of civil liberties on college campuses. But he was having difficulty getting some prominent faculty to sign. Walking home one evening from a seminar he asked the sociologist Daniel Bell why he thought he was encountering so much faculty resistance. Bell responded in Yiddish, "Marty be careful—*men ken geharget weren.*" (You can get killed).

Leo Kaplan became a mentor during my final years at Queens College. After I graduated, he too was forced to resign rather than testify before the Special Investigating Unit of the Board of Higher Education. Before resigning he gave the keynote speech at an annual Hillel event on a theme made popular by Edward R. Morrow entitled: "This I Believe." Although he was untenured, he boldly asserted that professors who had been members of the Communist Party could be good teachers.

Leo stirred my interest in labor economics and labor history. He regaled me with stories about organizing steel workers in Colorado, connecting those experiences with the role ordinary people played in advancing social and economic justice. At a time of political repression and conformity, Leo kept my utopian dreams alive. His own experiences as an organizer inspired me to pursue a master's degree in labor studies at the University of Illinois that I thought would provide the education I needed to participate more effectively in the labor movement.

Before departing to begin my graduate work, I was reminded how dangerous the political climate had become. On June 19, 1953, a week after I graduated from Queens College, Julius and Ethel Rosenberg were executed for spying for the Soviet Union. Was this the reason for Daniel Bell's warning? A few weeks later a man I had never met turned up at my Bronx apartment, claiming to be a representative of the Communist Party. I wondered whether I should talk to him. Who was he, and why did someone claiming to represent the Communist Party want to see me? Neighbors had already told me that FBI agents had questioned them about me. But after a brief exchange, and perhaps foolishly, I agreed to meet with him.

What happened next in retrospect seems absurd, almost farcical. After a summary of the Communist Party's recruiting efforts, he began speaking as if I was still a member, revealing that he had a special mission for me. The Communist Party wanted me to join other members who were organizing workers in the Detroit factories. I looked at him in disbelief. "I don't know who are. I'm not a member of the Communist Party. I plan to attend the University of Illinois in the fall. I'm not sure why you're here. I think it's time for you to leave." I still wonder whether he was a Communist Party activist or an agent of the FBI.

Gene Goodheart describes an exchange that took place in a class taught by the historian Richard Hofstadter in 1955. He recalls Hofstadter writing on the blackboard, *The history of all societies is the history of class cooperation.* Thinking that he had made mistake Gene asked, "Don't you mean class conflict?" Hofstadter must have enjoyed the moment. He smiled, responding that Marx was wrong. The history of class relations *was* primarily a history of class cooperation not class conflict.

I had similar experiences at the University of Illinois. My views about what workers and their unions wanted differed from those of my professors. During the Second World War many worked for the War Labor Board, seeking ways of fostering cooperation between management and workers. After the war, concerns about labor conflict accelerated as major strikes involving millions of workers erupted. In response to rising trade union power, the government passed the Taft Hartley Act, designed to constrain trade union clout, that included a provision requiring union leaders to file non-communist affidavits. Charges of communist influence were used to deflect and undermine trade union support. Under increasing legal and financial pressures, trade unions began purging communists from their ranks.

I rejected Hofstadter's argument and agreed with Marx that class conflict, not class cooperation, was the dominant attribute of worker–management relations. Most of my professors would have supported Hofstadter's views. Their research on the causes of worker management conflict were undertaken to help find ways of fostering greater labor management cooperation. I thought the competing interests of workers and their bosses made labor conflict inevitable. Strikes and other forms of resistance were essential means of improving worker's working conditions. The countervailing power of workers and their unions offered the best hope for improving the lives of workers.

Equalizing the power of workers and management might also

contribute to more responsible and fairer collective bargaining outcomes. In such an environment greater cooperation was more likely, and relations between trade unions and management could become less confrontational and bitter. Was my view different from either Hofstadter's or Marx's understanding of class conflict? Many years later I would address of some of these questions with the founders of the Swedish welfare state.

But I had already experienced what suppressed labor conflict felt like. In 1951 Ray and I found summer jobs working in an electrical equipment factory and warehouse. The friend who tipped us off about the job told us it would be better to appear stupid than smart in our interview. We followed his instructions, pretending some difficulty completing the simple job application. We were hired. But I sensed that this would be an eventful summer job, especially when the smiling manager said, "You boys look like nice kids, so I'm paying you five dollars a week more than most of the other workers. Do your work, and don't be troublemakers, and you will be OK."

Following his advice would not be easy. On the first day on the job, we were assigned to a group of five workers packing electrical supplies and carrying the boxes to a loading area. A foreman whose main task seemed to be harassing and prodding us to work faster made the boring work more difficult. As the day progressed, he became more aggressive, pushing and sometimes smacking workers across the face, calling one worker a stupid spic. When the worker turned around, he ran up to him, grabbed him between his legs, and shouted, "What are you going to do about it?" Ray and I left work that afternoon wondering how to respond. We felt powerless. It was clear that nothing could be done without the co-operation of other workers and ultimately a union.

The next day we began searching for workers who might join us in organizing some form of resistance. We each took on the task of finding workers we thought we could trust. By the third day we identified eight workers and invited them to meet with us during the lunch break. We wouldn't have much time to talk but we thought we could learn something about their grievances and whether we could enlist them in organizing a union.

To my surprise all the workers showed up. After introductions, Ray and I began to speak about what we had seen and experienced. I told them we were being paid more than they were. Why, I asked, would the boss do that unless he wanted to buy our cooperation and divide us?

Some of the workers began to speak about their work experiences. What we had seen, they said, was only a small sample of what they encountered, and they were under constant threat of being fired for any sign of slacking off. But then they shrugged and said, "There is nothing to be done. They run the show."

I responded, "There *is* something we can do. We can bring in a union."

There was an uncomfortable silence. I seemed to have crossed a line. One of the workers said, "That's dangerous. We could lose our jobs."

I pulled back. "Maybe we should think about it and meet again." They nodded, and we went back to work.

The workers were clearly fearful of managerial retribution. But without help from a union we could do very little to change working conditions. Ray and I decided to reach out to the United Electrical Workers Union during the weekend. The next day, before we entered the plant, someone yelled, "Silverman and Stollerman, come to the office!"

As soon as we entered the manager shut the door and began shouting, "You ungrateful commie bastards. You fucking troublemakers. I don't want to see your faces anywhere near our factory. Get the fuck out of my office."

Stunned, we quickly left. I turned to Ray and said, "There must have been an informer at our meeting. We didn't have a chance. Why did we talk about bringing in a union without knowing a lot more about whom we could trust?" We agonized about who the informer might be. We had a lot to learn about organizing workers.

I was clearly the outlier among the students and faculty at the Labor Institute. Only one other student expressed an interest in pursuing a career in the labor movement. Understanding the factors that contribute to labor management cooperation seemed to be a guiding purpose of the Institute. So I was intrigued by an announcement of a lecture by Professor Clark Kerr with the title: "The Positive Role of Conflict in Labor Management Relations."

I went to the lecture hoping to find support for my views about the nature of worker–management relations. I was only partly vindicated. Professor Kerr did not address the role of class conflict in the larger context of class relations. But he did affirm that labor conflict was a way workers revealed their grievances and a means of improving working conditions. Management benefited as well because, when workers felt they had a voice in determining the conditions of their employment, worker productivity improved. I understood Professor Kerr to mean that, individually, workers had limited power, but with the help of unions their voices could be heard, and as a result their loyalty to the firm would increase and labor turnover would decrease. I found the argument plausible but wondered why bosses would voluntarily limit their control of the work process.

My introduction to debates about the role of trade unions raised questions about their functions as agents of change. According to the economists John Commons and Selig Perlman, whose works I was then studying, trade unions were fundamentally conservative institutions with limited goals. Successful trade union leaders accepted the power of capitalists and their management of the modern economy. Unlike risk-taking capitalists with visions of unlimited opportunity, trade unions were more conscious of the limited job opportunities of workers. Job consciousness, not class consciousness, was the basis on which mature trade union action was built.

In Perlman's theory the intellectual played a particularly destructive role. In his telling, the intellectual underestimated the resistance power of capital and misread the behavior of workers, who were more concerned about what happened on the job than their class position. Since intellectuals had a political agenda, they were unable to accept the reality of worker's more limited interests. As a result, Perlman argued intellectuals were disruptive influences in the evolution of trade unions.

When I first encountered Perlman's theory of trade unions, I thought it was a political statement formulated as an objective theory. It certainly did not reflect the American and European experiences or my own contact with radical trade unionists. Comparative studies of trade unions suggested that some of the most successful unions had close ties to socialist and labor parties and promoted greater equality in the distribution of income and power. In my view, unlike that of Perlman, trade unions responded in a variety of ways to the challenges of capitalist development. I believed that labor unions played a major role in promoting values of social justice and worker solidarity. I also thought that intellectuals could help workers develop the knowledge and skills necessary to challenge the corporation's control over production. Many years later I developed an educational program to help enhance workers' capacity to participate more effectively in their unions and in the workplace—an experience that challenged my views about trade unions as agents of radical reform.

But I was also troubled by what became known as the historic compromise between labor and management. In 1950 General Motors and the United Automobile Workers Union agreed to cede control over production to GM in exchange for tying wages to productivity growth and changes in the cost of living. The agreement, called the Detroit Plan, contributed to the development of a private welfare system. Walter Reuther, the union president, proclaimed that the UAW had created a middle-income worker. I wondered whether the union's focus on middle-class consumption instead of greater worker control over production undermined norms of solidarity. Writing in *Fortune* magazine at the time, Daniel Bell confirmed my skepticism. He argued that "GM may have paid a billion dollars for peace, but it got a bargain. . . . The agreement. . .suggested that increases in wages were not determined by political power but rather by sharing the productivity gains of labor: not the conflict over the increasing surplus value created by labor but rather by the increasing productivity of workers."

Questions about what unions do were only part of the challenges I encountered at the University of Illinois. I remember a winter day in 1954 when I flippantly told a friend sitting near me in the library, "Charles, you need a haircut. Let's go downstairs to the barber shop and get our hair clipped."

Charles just smiled and continued reading. A New Orleans native, he was one of two Black students enrolled in the Institute. When I persisted, he turned and said, "Don't you know I can't get my haircut downstairs?" I was stunned and soon learned that barbershops around the University were not open to Black students, and that some students had begun to organize to end those blatant acts of discrimination.

Since the barbers were violating the Civil Rights Act of the State of Illinois, we devised a plan that would open the barbershops to all customers. We began enlisting students and faculty to help obtain evidence necessary to bring charges against the barbers for violating the Civil Rights Act. We employed a simple tactic. A white and a Black student were sent to a barbershop. If the barber cut the hair of the white student but refused to serve the black student, we had clear evidence of discrimination.

But barbers quickly realized what we were doing. When a Black student entered, they offered some perfunctory excuse and closed their shop. We succeeded in closing most of the barbershops in town, but we did not have sufficient evidence to bring the barbers to court.

We decided to modify our tactics. Instead of sending two students or faculty for haircuts, we sent three. After a white customer was attended to and a Black student denied service, we waited patiently for the barbershop to reopen. A white student or faculty member then entered and was served. The tactic worked. We finally had the evidence we needed that would make it possible for Black students to get haircuts on or near the University of Illinois campus.

I have a vivid memory of standing with Charles and a faculty member on the steps leading down to the barbershop near the Labor Institute. Professor Chalmers had volunteered to be the third person to enter the barbershop. He was clearly nervous but excited. Turning to me he said, "Bert, this is the most meaningful civil act I have engaged in since participating in the great auto strikes of the 1930s."

It was not the only time I confronted blatant racial discrimination in Champaign-Urbana Illinois. One incident remains vividly embedded in my memory. Evelyn and I, and two couples from the Labor Institute, met in a restaurant to celebrate the completion of our studies. One couple was Black and the other, with whom we had become very close, were Mormons. The husband, Boyd, a decorated Second World War air force pilot, was one of the other students at the Institute who planned to work for a trade union after graduation.

Deeply engrossed in conversation, I didn't realize that we weren't being served. When Boyd asked what I thought was happening, I decided to find out. I approached manager and asked why it was taking so long to be served. He stared menacingly at me and said, "I can serve you anywhere I want. I can serve you in the kitchen, I can serve in the bathroom, or I can serve you outside."

I responded contemptuously, warning, "We'll see about that." I returned to our table and explained what had happened. Outraged, Boyd suggested we confront the manager immediately. I reminded everyone that we did have an alternative. We could sit quietly and refuse to move, and if not served, we could file a discrimination complaint. Our Black friends responded hesitantly. They understood the importance of doing something but were worried that their participation might jeopardize the husband's State of Virginia scholarship. They hoped to return to Virginia the following month, and if what we planned became known, their family's safety might be at risk. Respecting their concerns, we quietly left the restaurant.

Race was not the only challenge I observed that year in Illinois. I also encountered anti-Semitism in an unexpected place. We lived in a low-income neighborhood. Evelyn and I had rented a studio apartment in a large house owned by a working-class family. The rental income enabled the wife to stay at home and care for their two children. We had little contact except for an occasional exchange of pleasantries, and therefore I was surprised when our landlord invited us to their family's Christmas Eve potluck dinner. Pleased, I said we would gladly come and asked what we could bring. John smiled and said, "Surprise us. Bring what you folks like to eat."

"Okay," I said. "We'll bring a taste of New York."

He hesitated for a moment and said, "Do you mean Jewish food?"

"We could do that" I replied, "but that's not the only cuisine New York is known for."

We didn't contribute a Jewish dish to the potluck dinner. Evelyn made an eggplant casserole that everyone seemed to like. It was a warm, festive evening. After dinner we sang Christmas carols, and I had an opportunity to talk to John about growing up in Champaign-Urbana. He learned that he had lived in Urbana all his life and, like his dad, worked in the University's maintenance department. He liked the job but not the bureaucrats who made his work more difficult.

As the guests began to leave, he turned to me and said, "Hey, Bert, come with me—I need to get something in town. I'm sure your wife won't mind."

Surprised, I wondered what to make of this sudden intimacy. We got into his truck and drove a few miles to a local hardware store. We were about to get out of the car when he turned to me and said, "I hope you don't mind my asking, but it's been on my mind all evening." He hesitated for a moment and then asked, "Is it true that Jews have little tails?"

Shocked I said, "Are you joking? I can pull down my pants so you can get a good look at my ass."

He started laughing uneasily taken aback by my response. "Look", he said, "it was something that my friends and I were told when we were kids. I didn't believe it, but many of my friends did."

Stunned I said, "At some level you must have believed it. Otherwise, why would you ask?" I wasn't sure what else to say. Was his bluntness a way of reaching out to me? His friendliness and warmth during the potluck dinner suggested that he was trying to establish a neighborly connection. "Look," I went on, "I never thought you were an anti-Semite. You're a nice guy, and I hope we can be friends. Besides, you're my landlord." He laughed, and we shook hands.

Five years later I would, once again, encounter anti-Semitism but a more subtle and consequential variety.

I returned to New York in September 1954, greeted by the long-dreaded news I had done so much to avoid. Not only had I been drafted into the U.S. Army, but I also had to make a difficult decision. All recruits, before beginning their service, were required to sign a loyalty oath. All my friends confronted the same problem. Should we sign or refuse? In a period of anti-communist hysteria, either political choice carried its own risks.

Like most of my friends I decided to sign the oath. The dire consequences of that decision would haunt us during our years of service.

While my army experiences had moments of farce, at times it felt perilously life-changing. Waiting on line at the induction center to receive my army identification number, I did not realize that the soldier standing not far behind me had a similar name and, except for the last two digits, would be given an identical serial number. But in most other respects Bertrand Silverman and I were not alike. He was tall, heavy-set, awkward, and withdrawn. But our virtually identical names and serial numbers would keep us closely linked for the next sixteen weeks.

I first encountered him when a sergeant began reading a list of names of soldiers designated to go to Fort Ord, California, for basic training. I turned in disbelief when he shouted Bertrand Silverman's name. Even the sergeant paused for a moment, wondering if he had made a mistake. We were assigned to the same barracks, and he slept in a bunk bed below me. We never developed a close friendship. He had difficulty relating to other soldiers, spending most of his free time alone, while I began forming relationships that would play an important role in shaping my life in the army.

It is difficult to motivate individuals with different biographies to cooperate in achieving common objectives. The U.S. Army had a special way of loosening primary bonds that might weaken a soldier's willingness to follow rules and obey the commands of their superiors. The sergeant who greeted us outside our barracks asked in a folksy, Southern twang, "I hear that you New York boys are very smart. I need to choose some soldiers for a special assignment that requires special skills. Tell me, how many of you have a college degree?" A majority raised their hands. Smiling, he asked them to step forward and then asked, "Do any of you have more than a college degree? If so step forward and join the other smart boys."

I joined the smaller but still significant number of soldiers and stepped forward. Then he mockingly shouted, "I want all you smart boys to drop down on your knees and slowly move forward, picking up any piece of paper or cigarette butt you see in the area in front of the barracks." He turned to the rest of the group and yelled, "Now, you dumb bastards watch and learn how it's done."

So began my initiation into army life. We learned to chant and march in unison and to follow the sergeant's cadence and commands. He tried, as I've said, to weaken primary attachments that might undermine his authority. I remember a special exercise we did to promote loyalty. Commanding us to hold our rifles with our arms fully extended, he shouted, "Who do you hate?" It's very difficult to hold a rifle in that position for an extended period, but not to do so would result in more abuse. We also knew what he wanted us to shout. We had practiced the routine in the barracks. Responding weakly at first, we shouted, "I hate my mother."

"Louder!" he commanded.

I couldn't hold my rifle in that position much longer. In a rage I shouted, "I hate my mother."

He then shouted, "And who do you love?"

We shouted in unison, "I love my sergeant."

Such transparent efforts seemed silly and counterproductive and only increased my contempt for his abusive authority. I was fortunate that Spurt, a friend from the Bronx who was part of my unit, also happened to be a skilled boxer. He had his own way of undermining the sergeant's power. Spurt's glare or delayed response to an order invited laughter. Enraged, our sergeant finally challenged him to settle their differences privately. It was a bad decision. Spurt thrashed him, and he was soon replaced. No one spoke about the incident, but Spurt had earned everyone's admiration. I benefited as well. In his company I had a respected guardian.

Despite my disdain for the army's methods of promoting loyalty, I did feel something familiar as we marched past our commanding officer in a ceremony marking the end of our basic training. Was this the same state of mind I experienced while participating in my first May Day parade? I had been seven years old then, and all the children had been dressed in white. I'd felt a rush of excitement as we marched and chanted slogans I have long forgotten. But I still remember the sensation of feeling a part of something larger than myself. Those responses returned as I marched on that final day of basic training.

Of my many memories of army life, few invoke greater anxiety of impending disaster than the possible discovery of my communist past. There was a moment toward the end of basic training when we assembled in a large auditorium to hear an officer speak about the dangers of Chinese communism. When the lecture ended, a friend seated next to me raised his hand. At first the officer ignored him, but Larry insisted on being heard. Finally, the officer shouted, "Soldier do you have a question you want to ask?"

Larry rose slowly from his seat and boldly asserted, "Sir, I don't think you have given us a complete picture of the Chinese Revolution and its significance for the Chinese people." Without waiting for a response Larry began citing the Chinese Revolution's many accomplishments. He didn't get very far. The officer cut him off and asked for his name and serial number. Then, addressing us, he sneered, "Evidently, this soldier forgot he was no longer in a college classroom. In the army we confront life-and-death issues. China is a threat to our security, and you need to know what we're up against."

As we left the auditorium, I saw Larry walking slowing ahead of me. I tried to keep my distance, thinking it best to talk to him later when we were alone. I needed time to assess what had happened. Larry's behavior had implications not only for him but also for me. We were more than army buddies. Larry's wife Sonya was a friend of my wife, and they had decided to join us. They'd rented a house in Pacific Grove not too far from the base, so we might spend weekends together. It was a small, inexpensive bungalow, easily affordable when shared. It was evident to many soldiers that Larry and I had a special relationship.

I could hardly contain my anger when we found time to meet. Distressed I shouted, "Why did you do that? What did you think you could accomplish? What's your plan now? What do you think will happen to you and to me?"

He shook his head and replied, "I'm sorry. I just couldn't sit there and listen to the crap he was feeding us."

I'm not sure what I said next, but I remember muttering, "We can no longer spend any time together."

A few days later I learned he had been interviewed by counter-intelligence officers and had been sent back to Fort Dix, New Jersey. I thought I would soon be summoned for questioning. Soldiers who bunked near me were called in for interviews. At one point one of those soldiers asked, "Bert, are you Bertram or Bertrand Silverman? I never could get your names straight."

I smiled and said, "What's up?" He must have caught the edge in my voice because he shrugged off my question, saying he was just curious.

All of this happened during the final days of our training. Fortunately, I knew the soldier who was working on the orders for our next posting. I reached out to him, saying, "Anything but Korea would be great."

He nodded and said, "I'll see what I can do." It was not until later that day that I remembered the other Bert. I ran to the office, found the soldier responsible for our next assignment, and I told him I was worried he might confuse me with the another Bert Silverman. He shrugged and said that our orders had been set and there was nothing more he could do.

What happened next only heightened my anxiety. I learned that I had been assigned to the Army Chemical Center, located outside of Baltimore, Maryland. Why, I wondered, was I being sent to a high security army base? Bewildered and confused, my paranoia on full throttle, thoughts of the Rosenbergs flashed through my mind. It was not until I returned home that another, more benign possibility emerged. Perhaps this was the result of my friend's effort to keep me from being sent to Korea. Those were soothing thoughts, but they did not ease the fears that haunted my time at the Army Chemical Center. A few days after arriving, I realized that my only defense against exposure was to become invisible. I discovered that I had one of the four positions that did not require a security clearance. I needed to hold on to my job.

To be anonymous made it impossible to establish relationships with soldiers or civilians who worked on the army base—not an easy task when you are a part of a close-knit community. It was especially difficult during the first few weeks before I moved off base. The soldiers in my company were bright young men seeking connections and friendships. While affable, I spent my free time carefully avoiding conversations about work-related activities. Keeping a low profile was easier after Evelyn and I moved into a Baltimore apartment.

Living in Baltimore significantly reduced the time I spent on the army base. I soon fell into a routine of arriving at work at nine in the morning and leaving at five. The job of managing the personnel records of the soldiers assigned to the base was not very demanding. It consumed only half a day of my work. But I was forbidden to do anything outside of my assigned duties. I found sitting idly at my desk boring, so I violated my effort to be invisible. I started reading a book. But not any book. I began reading the bible.

I placed the bible on my lap, moving my chair slightly away from my desk. I kept an eye on the warrant officer seated on a raised platform, monitoring our work. I thought I could read a few paragraphs and then check on the officer to avoid detection

For a few weeks it worked until one afternoon an angry voice shouted, "Soldier, what are you reading?"

I looked up and saw my commanding officer glaring at me. I jumped to my feet with the book in my hand and shouted, "The bible, sir."

He stared at the book. His demeanor abruptly changed. Smiling he put his hand on my shoulder and said, "Keep reading, soldier. Faith is a powerful weapon."

I sat down still holding the bible and for a moment felt safe. A few weeks later, he summoned me to his office. Looking my personnel file, he said, "Silverman, I'm transferring you to another unit where you will be given more responsibilities and greater opportunities for promotion."

My response surprised and confused him. "Sir," I shouted, "why would you do this? I like working with you. I'm not concerned about getting promoted. It's the job, not the rank, that is important to me. I appreciate your concern, but don't transfer me to another assignment."

Surprised, he exclaimed, "Silverman I'm trying to help you."

I nodded. "Yes, I know, sir, but I want to work with you."

He shook his head and said, "OK, if that's what you want."

I left his office feeling relieved and humiliated. I had escaped exposure but been forced to act like a fool. I began to doubt my decision to sign the loyalty oath, vowing never to put myself in that position again.

Those sentiments were confirmed by friends who, unlike me, did not escape the repressive force of the army. Ray was picked up by the military police in the middle of the night while on maneuvers in Germany and brought before a general who berated him for his disloyalty. Another friend, Simms Taback, while at Fort Meade, Maryland, was grilled for ten hours, floodlights glaring in his face. Each had endured harrowing experiences of interrogation and threats of imprisonment. Ray's company commander, in a rage, shouted, "Soldier, if it was up to me, I would hang you from a lamppost along with all the other commie bastards."

Their experiences heightened my sense of imminent danger. My body stiffened whenever a soldier from army counterintelligence approached my desk, wondering if he was coming for me.

Despite these troubling moments, I began exploring opportunities for pursuing a Ph.D. in economics after my army service ended. The University of California at Berkeley's economics program, and their Institute of Industrial Relations, seemed like an ideal choice. My professors at the University of Illinois encouraged me to apply. Returning to the San Francisco area made this choice especially attractive. It was the only graduate school application I submitted.

The letter from the Berkeley came three months later. Reading it renewed feelings of new possibilities. Not only had I been accepted to the Ph.D. program, but I had also been awarded a research assistantship. The financial support, and the GI Bill, were more than enough to fund my studies. I began imagining life after the army.

A few weeks later, those dreams were shattered. A second letter from University of California arrived, enclosed in a larger envelope with employment forms that new employee needed to complete. One changed everything. The University was requiring that I sign a loyalty oath. My heart sank. I had sworn never to sign such an oath again. I needed more time to decide what to do. I called Leo Kaplan for advice.

Leo, a victim of McCarthyism, had recently been forced to leave his Queens College teaching position. I should have anticipated his response. "Why do you want to put yourself through the same experience you had in the army? You're a New York Jew interested in the labor movement and socialism. You'll be a likely target." I decided to decline Berkeley's offer and applied instead for admission to Columbia University. I was accepted but too late to apply for any financial support. Resentful, I turned my attention to completing my army service. Nothing prepared me for what happened next.

On June 5, 1956, the *New York Times* published the secret speech Nikita Khrushchev had given to the 20th Congress of the Soviet Communist Party. I read it, enraged. "All lies, all lies!" I shouted at the walls in my Baltimore apartment. I remember thinking this was not the full story. Stalin could not be solely responsible for such treachery. They all had blood on their hands.

I had left the Communist Party in 1950 because its top-down decision making restricted political debate and dialogue. And yet

I still believed that the Party's hierarchical structure and secrecy were a necessary response to McCarthyism and the Smith Act. Khrushchev's speech changed all that. Exposed were acts of repression, treachery, and murder in the name of socialism. Most of my friends who had become Party members responded with their feet. They joined more than 30,000 American communists who left the Party that year. The 20th Congress report marked the end of the Communist Party as political actor in the United States.

At first, I simply lashed out in anger. I questioned my own complicity. Why had I been so blind? I had raised questions about the 1930s Soviet trials and convictions of communist leaders. But despite my doubts, I'd accepted the answers I received from family, friends, and teachers sympathetic to Soviet socialism. Their arguments were always the same: Stalinist policies were necessary responses to a hostile capitalist world. Without the heroic resistance of Soviet forces, we would not have won the war against fascism.

My initial reaction to the Khrushchev speech began to change. Were my socialist values wanting, or my failure to apply them when evaluating socialist practices? There could no longer be any double standards. Socialist values should apply equally in building socialism and in criticizing capitalism. I could not abandon the values that had guided my visions of a more just and caring society and the community of friends that shared those values.

In his essay in the book *The God That Failed*, Ignazio Silone captures some of those sentiments:

> The day I left the Communist Party. . .was a day of
> deep mourning, the mourning of my lost youth. . . . But

my faith in Socialism. . .has remained more than ever in me. In its essence, it has gone back to what it was when I first revolted against the social order. . .an affirmation of the human person over all the economic and social mechanisms which oppress him. . . . I do not conceive of Socialism as tied to any particular theory, but to a faith. The more socialist theories claim to be "scientific" the more transitory they are, but socialist values are permanent. . . . On a group of theories one can found a school; but on a group of values one can found a culture . . .a new way of living among men.

Over the next few years, I encountered many disillusioned communists. I remember a chance encounter with Chaver Gellman, who had asked me to recite Yiddish poems at various events sponsored by the Jewish People's Fraternal Order. One of the poems I recited was Itzhik Feffer's, *"Zug Ich Stalin"* proclaiming Stalin's virtues: *"Zug ich Stalin main ich gut, zug ich Stalin main ich mut."* (When I speak of Stalin, I mean good, when I speak of Stalin. I mean courage). Chaver Gellman grabbed me and, before I could say anything, that soft-spoken man began to shout, "Bert, I picked up Feffer's book of poems and I ripped them out page by page! How could we have *been* so blind?"

Brief encounters with some prominent communists revealed how profoundly a crisis of belief had consumed the leadership of the Communist Party. I met Joseph Starobin, the former foreign editor of the Communist Party newspaper, the *Daily Worker,* while searching for a summer rental in the Berkshires. The Starobins had converted a large silo into a house with unusual features, including a circular metal staircase originally used in a submarine. When it became clear that the house would not serve our needs, I shifted the conversation and asked about his work as a foreign correspondent. Suddenly his demeanor changed, and he bitterly exclaimed that everything he wrote was edited to conform to Soviet foreign policy. He too then shook his head and said, "All lies, all lies."

I met the novelist Howard Fast before Khrushchev's historic speech. It was the second week of June 1952, while Evelyn and I were vacationing at the Fur Workers Union's resort. Among the guests were four Communist leaders who, I later learned, planned to go underground to avoid imprisonment under the Smith Act. Fast asked us to watch his young son while he spoke to guests on the theme, "Why There Was No Anti-Semitism in the Soviet Union." I learned later that in 1949 Paul Novick, the editor of the *Morning Freiheit*, had informed Fast about the arrests and execution of Jewish writers. Fast waited until 1957 to express his anguish after reading Khrushchev's speech. "I was filled with loathing and disgust. I felt a sense of unmitigated mental nausea at the realization that I had supported and defended this murderous bloodbath."

I never met John Gates, who at the age of twenty-four fought in the Spanish Civil War, reaching the rank of commissar in the American Abraham Lincoln brigade. But our lives intersected in an unexpected way. Gates had devoted his life to the Communist Party. After the revelation of the horrors of Soviet repression, he tried to use his influence within the Party, and his voice as editor of the *Daily Worker*, to change Communist Party policies. His failed efforts to reform the Communist Party finally led to his resignation in January 1958. In that year John Gates took over my job as a research assistant for the International Garment Workers Union.

For the historian Eric Hobsbawm as well as for some of my friends, the Communist Party was more than just another political organization. Leaving was akin to severing ties with their most intimate relationships. I remember my friend Stretch's words when we met in New York at the end of my army service. Dismissing my anger about Soviet treachery he exclaimed, "When I meet with my brothers and sisters in the Party, we simply embrace and understand that the fight must go on."

Mom too had difficulty reconciling her idealized view of Soviet Union. Hers was a more painful path. As we sat around the kitchen table, she looked at me and said, "The Russians are good people. Look how bravely they fought to defeat the Nazis. How many lost their lives to save us from fascism. They will change things and correct Stalin's mistakes."

"Mom," I yelled, "I *read* the speech, you didn't! The crimes could not have been the work of one man. Many hands are dirty."

She shook her head and, in a soft voice, began to repeat a familiar refrain: "Don't worry. Things will get better. The Soviet people want a better life."

But things did not get better. The world of her imagination began to crumble. Friendships were broken. Her faith in a radiant future began to dissolve. It was two in the morning when the phone rang. It was my father. He was crying. "Bert, I don't know what to do. Help me. It's Mom. She's hysterical."

"Let me speak to her," I said.

Her voice frightened me. "Bertram, help me, help me. I can't go on. I don't want to live."

During the next few weeks, we searched for professional help. I finally found a psychiatrist associated with Cornell University who agreed to see her.

His assessment was not reassuring. He told us that Mom was suicidal and needed to be hospitalized for assessment and treatment. The psychiatrist recommended electro-shock therapy as the most effective way to address her depression. At first, I resisted but after consultations with others, I reluctantly agreed to go ahead with the procedure.

It seemed to work. She no longer showed symptoms of depression or anxiety. But she was no longer the mother I knew. Gone was the agitated vitality that so touched me as a child. Gone was that critical edge that had kept alive her search for something beyond her current circumstances now replaced by a passive calmness and resignation. Increasingly, she retreated into her own thoughts. She was no longer anxious or depressed, but she had lost her soul.

As she aged, there were times when glimmers of the mother I knew resurfaced. One vivid moment stands out. She was 92 years old, living alone in an assisted living unit in the Bronx. Alice and I invited her to a Passover Seder. I suggested we edit the reading of the Haggadah because I believed my mother would lose patience with the more traditional rendition of the Passover story. She did not follow my advice. I watched as Mom lifted her four-foot, ten-inch frame and, turning to Alice said, "Thank you for a wonderful dinner. But let me say something about the true meaning of Passover not disclosed in your Haggadah. Passover is not only a story about Jewish liberation. It is also story about freedom for the Palestinians."

And then turning to the guests in the room, including my daughter's Irish boyfriend, she continued, "It is also about freedom for the Irish and the South Africans and all groups seeking justice and liberty." It is the last memory I have of my mother. She died the following year.

My army career ended on July 28, 1956—but not without an anxious but somewhat amusing finality. It was my last day of work at the Army Chemical Center. I sat at my desk, finishing the transfer orders for a soldier going to Fort Dix, New Jersey, for discharge from the army. As I typed the necessary forms, I thought that perhaps the worst was finally over.

Suddenly I heard a woman's voice shouting as she approached my desk. "Look, there's Bert Silverman, from Camp Kinderland!"

I put my head down not knowing how to react but quickly realized that the word Kinderland meant nothing to those seated around me. She was the wife of the soldier whose file I had been working on. I had forgotten her name. We exchanged some pleasantries and spoke briefly about people we knew. When they left, I realized I was no longer the person she thought I was when she yelled, "Bert Silverman from Camp Kinderland."

Chapter 4

FINDING SOCIALISM

THE ECONOMIST JOHN KENNETH GALBRAITH, reflecting on the changing social and political climate of the 1950s, wrote discouragingly that American liberals and social democrats had assumed that:

> the newly affluent blue-collar worker with middle income (as well as other white-collar and professional groups), protected from the trials of unemployment, old-age and illness would in gratitude have political attitudes different from those of the older rich. . . Liberals were wrong.

Capitalism's achievements and the revelation of Soviet communism's failures posed challenging questions about the future of socialism. I hoped Columbia University might offer opportunities to explore feasible alternatives to capitalism. I believed that a social democratic path to socialism was still possible. Such subjects were no longer important to my friends, who had become more involved with their careers and families.

Through these portals no mortals shall walk. Those words light up whenever I walk through Columbia University's gates. For many students Columbia would be the beginning of a seemingly endless road to complete their doctoral studies. Many would leave empty-handed. It did not take long for me to realize that the Columbia economics department was not an ideal place to pursue my search for new ways of organizing how we worked and lived.

When I applied for admission, I did not realize that Columbia accepted many more students for their doctoral program than they thought would finish. Many would drop out after a year or two, some settling for a master's degree. At the initial orientation I learned little about the department's goals, nor did I sense any interest in developing a learning community. With little guidance from the faculty, students pursued their own paths to complete their studies. Many courses could be taken for attendance credit. After qualifying in econometrics and one other subject area, and showing competence in two languages, the final challenge entailed passing an oral examination in four subjects. Only then could you begin the research and ultimately the defense of your doctoral dissertation. Few students had the resources to complete their studies without working. For many it would take almost a decade to complete the requirements.

I remember my classmate Robert Fogel's advice: "Choose a

subject for a master's essay that you can turn into a doctoral dissertation. It's the best way to reduce the time it takes to complete your doctorate." I had met Bob at the departmental orientation. I knew him from my past political life. He had been a leader of the Labor Youth League, an organization affiliated with the Communist Party. Many years later he would win the Nobel Prize in Economics.

Bob had clearly abandoned his communist past. He showed little interest in radical politics or Marxist theory. We took classes in economic theory with William Vickery, who would also win the Nobel Prize in economics, and econometrics courses with Frederick Mills. Bob never raised questions about traditional economic theory, focusing primarily on his grades. He often quibbled over test results with the graduate assistant in our statistics course. I understood his concerns about his grades. His father was paying his tuition and providing financial support for him and his family. Bob left Columbia at the end of the academic year for Johns Hopkins University when Columbia failed to offer him a fellowship to complete his studies.

I thought I had found a kindred spirit when Jimmy Weinstein joined our luncheon conversations. Jimmy and Bob were friends both active in radical politics during their student days at Cornell University. Like Bob, Jimmy had left the Communist Party in 1956 and come to Columbia to pursue a doctorate in American history. Unlike Bob he still professed an interest in socialism. Jimmy never completed his doctoral studies. I remember a conversation we had outside the main reading room of the New York Public Library, just before he left Columbia. When I asked about his current research, he spoke about research on American liberalism. But then he said, smiling, that he was thinking of starting a business building sailboats.

Jimmy had more options than most of us. He was independently wealthy and chose a different path than the one Bob took. He decided to use his wealth and knowledge to promote socialist values and ideas. He helped fund and found the journals *Studies on the Left* and *Socialist Revolution*, as well as the newspaper *In These Times*. He had found a way of fighting for a socialist future. I had more limited aspirations as I sought to discover a path through the Columbia curriculum that provided a deeper understanding of capitalist development and its alternatives.

I remember sitting next to Bob when Professor Vickery introduced us to the foundations of economic theory. The class setting was unusual, as was his teaching method. At the beginning of each class, Professor Vickery placed a tape recorder on his desk and began speaking, thereby denying any opportunity for student discussions and questions. It soon became clear that taping his lectures were part of Professor Vickery's efforts to publish a textbook on economic theory. He distributed mimeographed versions of each chapter as they were completed. They provided a handbook on the technical underpinning of neo-classical economic theory. But the social and economic institutions on which the theory rested were never explored. Nor were we given an opportunity to debate the underlying values on which the theory rested. This became evident when explaining the distribution of income between workers and bosses.

He introduced us to a theory of income determination developed by John Bates Clarke, a former Columbia University professor. The theory became the established critique of Karl Marx's claim that the labor market concealed the source of capitalist profits and the exploitation of workers. Clarke contended that a natural law guided the distribution of income. If markets for labor and capital were free from outside interference, workers and bosses would receive an income equal to the amount of value they created. Under such conditions, the different classes would have no grievances against each other. He confidently asserted, "If nothing suppresses competition, progress will continue forever." Clarke's theory was more a vision of a capitalist utopia than a guide to how labor markets worked in a capitalist society.

My own experiences suggested that labor was not like any other commodity. Wages, and the conditions of work, depended on the worker's relative power in the workplace and on the economic and cultural conditions in which labor markets were embedded. Clarke's theory provided no role for workers and their unions to change the conditions of their labor or to imagine an alternative future.

It was when we turned to the study of macroeconomics that we began to address problems of capitalism's instability. And yet the Keynes to which we were introduced bore little resemblance to the rebel who had caused such a stir among economists. Keynes was presented as a social engineer rather than a radical reformer. But it was Keynes' radical and utopian vision that captured my imagination.

Challenging the faith in free markets, Keynes called for "a somewhat comprehensive socialization of investment" to ensure greater economic security and stability. And he warned that "the ideas of economists and political philosophers, both when they are right and when they are wrong, are more powerful than is commonly understood. Indeed, the world is ruled by little else." I found Keynes' explanation of capitalist instability enlightening because it offered possibilities for reform, and his vision of the future inspired my utopian yearnings.

In an article entitled "Letter to My Grandchildren," Keynes imagined a time in the not-too-distant future when a new era of abundance would be born, guided by different values and sensibilities, a time when the pursuit of profit and the accumulation of wealth would no longer be highly valued.

Keynes reopened a question raised by Karl Marx. Like other economists writing at the time, Marx had argued that labor was the key creator of value. In contrast to neo-classical economists' contention that the value of goods and services depended on the subjective wants and desires of consumers, Keynes suggested that what we value, and the prices set by markets, are quite different since corporations have the power to shape our desires and wants.

But we never discussed such issues at Columbia.

As the academic year unfolded, I began to question my decision to pursue a Ph.D. Some Columbia faculty contributed to my doubts. I walked into Professor Dorfman's class on the history of economic thought with great anticipation. Dorfman had written what was considered the definitive biography of Thorstein Veblen. I thought his course might provide a broader and more critical perspective on the evolution of economic ideas and theories. To my surprise, only five students had enrolled in the class. At first, I thought this would encourage more discussion and the exchange of ideas. I was mistaken. Seated behind a desk and reading from a prepared text, Professor Dorfman began the class as if speaking to a large audience.

I stopped attending after listening to a few of his lectures, not because they were uninteresting, but because I discovered that his lectures were virtually identical to the ones given by Wesley Mitchell, his former Columbia teacher. Since I had a copy of those recent lectures, I decided to leave Dorfman's class and join Leo Wolman's labor economics seminar.

It was not a good choice. Professor Wolman's research on trade union growth and development was one of the reasons I decided to enroll in his course: Early in his career Wolman had directed research for the Amalgamated Clothing Workers Union. I did not know at the time that he would shortly retire. This probably accounted for the way he conducted the seminar. Much of our time was spent listening to reflections about his experiences in government and in the labor movement.

It became evident from his negative comments about the role of unions in the economy that Wolman's sympathies for trade unions had changed. There was a moment early in the seminar when I asked his opinion about a theory of trade union growth that had been recently published in the *American Economic Review*. He shrugged, responded that he knew nothing about Horace Davis, the author of the article, and didn't think much of his theory. I was taken aback by the dismissive remark and began to wonder whether coming to Columbia had been a mistake.

The economics department had been changing, moving from

a more institutional and historical approach to an emphasis on neo-classical economic theory. Fortunately, the courses I took in the economic history of Europe with Professor David Landes did provide opportunities for a more expansive understanding of economic and social change. Professor Landes' energy and engagement were a breath of fresh air. The course opened questions about the social and economic costs of industrialization in 19th-century Europe. Landes also introduced me to two economists who had rekindled debates about the future of socialism.

Karl Polanyi's *The Great Transformation* revealed that when labor, nature, and money were treated like any other commodity, then how we lived, worked, and the environment we inhabited became linked to the uncertainty and vagaries of the marketplace. Consequently, unfettered capitalism threatened, not only our livelihood, but the natural environment on which our very existence depended. To prevent such costly consequences, government regulation was an essential response to mitigate the injuries of capitalism.

In his *Capitalism and the Historians,* Friedrich Hayek disputed the prevailing views of historians that industrialization had imposed enormous social costs on an emerging working class. Those views, he claimed, reflected the socialist bias of historians who believed that an evolving capitalism had been detrimental to the working class. I did not know at the time that Hayek's book was of part of a crusade to defend capitalism against its critics and the emerging threat of socialism. Despite their opposing views I credit Polanyi and Hayek for posing questions that rekindled my interests in problems of social reform and radical change. What were the social and economic costs of social change? How have socialist revolutions dealt with those costs? Is reform rather than revolution a more sustainable and humane way of achieving socialist ideals?

As the academic year ended, such lofty questions were replaced by more personal concerns. There was a not-so-subtle pressure from family and friends to find a job and start a family. It was a moment when people were turning away from political engagements and focusing more on family and work. Years of relative deprivation had given way to a splurge of spending. Consuming had become the driving force of the economy. For many of my working-class friends, new opportunities for social mobility provided a path to participation in an emerging consumer culture. It was difficult to resist.

Thomas Mann wrote that "time cools, time clarifies, no mood can be maintained unaltered through the course of hours." But some sentiments are so deeply embedded in the fabric of social life that it is difficult to image how they might change. I too was initially caught up in the seductive and expanding consumer culture. I remember speaking to friends and family about finding land on which to build prefabricated homes. Was this a reflection of my utopian dreams or my way of submitting to the alure of an affluent society?

With so much effort devoted to finding a profession and starting a family, acquiring things assumed a special place in the lives of ordinary people. Symbols of success were encoded in the house you owned, the car you drove, and the flood of mass-produced goods that were altering household work. Memories of the icebox of our childhood, and Mom cleaning our laundry in the bathtub and drying clothes on a clothesline outside my bedroom window, were now reflections of a distance past. The consumer culture offered an escape from the poverty and deprivation we had experienced.

Yet I felt uneasy. It wasn't that I didn't want those objects that greatly improved how we lived, but I was troubled by how much effort and time the quest for more consumed. It changed our conversations and limited our political and civic engagements. A character in a John Updike novel muses that "we were all brought up to want things and maybe the world isn't big enough for all that wanting." Half in jest, I began telling my friends, "Want less, get more." At that moment it was no more than a gesture reflecting my disappointment with the way my world was changing. There seemed to be fewer opportunities for enjoying the simple pleasures of life.

Ambivalent about the course of my studies, I decided to take a leave of absence from Columbia and explore possible job opportunities. I wrote to some of the faculty I knew at the University of Illinois for help finding a job. I told them that my main goal was to work for a trade union. The letter I received from Professor Robin Fleming, the director of the Labor Relations Institute and soon to become President of the University of Michigan, surprised me. He suggested I consider another route. In a warm and generous letter, he recommended I explore a position working for a large corporation. A good friend was the vice-president and director of human resources at American Airlines. He had spoken to him about me and was certain he would see me. At first, I dismissed the idea. But I needed a job. Why not see what it entailed? I called and set up a meeting.

The American Airlines building was in midtown Manhattan. I took the elevator to the top floor and approached the receptionist. She smiled when I mentioned my name. She told me I was expected. The office of the vice-president (I have forgotten his name) was imposing, a conference table on one side and a couch and chairs on the other side. He greeted me as I approached his large desk at the far end of the office. Smiling, he acknowledged that his friend Robin had spoken to him about me, and that as a special favor he had agreed to see me.

What happened next startled me. Without warning, his demeanor changed. He began on an extended discourse on what human resource managers do, ending his lengthy sermon exclaiming that it would take extensive job experience to become fully qualified. And then, smiling, he sat back in his chair and went on, "American Airlines is not the place to get such training. You should try Macy's or Gimbel's, where all their services are contained within one building."

There was a moment of silence. I tried to conceal my anger. Did he think I was a fool, or was he having fun at my expense? He smiled again as I rose, somewhat dismissively stated, "I understand what you're suggesting," and quickly left, outraged at his not-so-subtle anti-Semitism. A few weeks later I found a job not too far from Macy's. I began working for the International Ladies Garment Workers' Union.

I did not need a recommendation from the Labor Institute to get the job. I did get some help from someone with close ties to the union's leadership. The reference came from Paul Levitas, the editor of *The New Leader*—a magazine sympathetic to trade unions and to social democratic politics. His recommendation was a favor to my father-in-law, who delivered his laundry.

My interview for a position in the research department could not have been more unlike my experience at American Airlines. I sensed the difference when entering the union's main headquarters on Broadway and 56th Street. Ordinary workers shared the elevator that took me to the union's research department. I walked into their office and was immediately introduced to its director.

Lazar Tepper, an intense man, was uninterested in any small talk. After a brief discussion about the ILGWU, he said, "You clearly have the credentials for the job, but I need some additional evidence." He reached for a printed sheet of paper on his desk. "All our research assistants must take this test. When you're done, we can talk more fully about the job." Surprised, I sat at a desk outside his office and completed the twenty questions intended to test my statistical skills. Teper quickly reviewed my answers, nodded his approval, and said, "Come in next Monday for an orientation about the union and the work of our department." The salary was a modest seventy-five dollars a week. It didn't matter. I was now a part of the labor movement.

It would not take too much time before my romantic ideals faded. The limited intellectual discourse within the department soon became apparent. There was virtually no opportunity for sharing ideas about the ILGWU and trade unions more generally. Our days were spent writing reports, providing information on the garment industry, preparing statistical data to assist with collective bargaining and legislative initiatives, and assisting members with unemployment insurance problems. There was much to learn, but the limitations of the job soon became apparent.

Walter Mankoff, the senior research assistant, symbolized in demeanor and behavior the qualities of a typical bureaucrat. He was primarily concerned with pleasing Teper, who in turn reacted quickly to the requests of David Dubinsky or D.D. as he was typically called. I remember a moment while sitting in Teper's office when his secretary told him that Dubinsky wanted to speak to him. Before answering the phone, he got up from his chair and put on his jacket, as if he had to be properly dressed before taking the call. Such behavior troubled me. Walter discouraged intellectual engagement and critical thinking about larger social and economic questions that might impact the union. I was left on my own to explore the role the union played in the industry and the economy. What I discovered challenged many of my beliefs about what trade unions do.

The ILGWU was then an organization of 450,000 thousand members that wielded considerable power in the garment industry and the larger society. It had used its influence to change the structure of the ladies' garment industry. By participating in regulating competition in an industry known for its sweatshops and poverty wages, the union helped create greater stability in the industry, significantly improving the standard of living of its workers. In its early history, socialists and communists helped build and lead the union and engaged in political battles for control.

Trade unions cherish their heroic histories that inspire loyalty and allegiance to the union. I was given books and articles about the ILGWU to connect me to key moments in the union's history: the uprising of the 20,000, a 1909 strike fueled by a teenager named

Clara Lemlich, followed by the infamous Triangle Shirtwaist Fire that exposed the dangerous working conditions of immigrant workers. From the small sweatshops, the 65-hour work week, and the poverty wages, a union led by socialists and communists had helped transform the garment industry and the working conditions of workers. I admired these achievements. But over time the union's linkages to the industry and its employers tended to isolate the leaders from its changing workforce. Their more elevated status and income increasingly separated them from the rank-and-file members they represented.

Many years later Doug Fraser, the president of the United Automobile Workers, laughed as he related how everyone claimed to be in The Battle of the Overpass in 1937 when Walter Reuther clashed with security guards during the strike at the Ford's River Rouge Plant Complex at Dearborn, Michigan. The older ILGWU leaders also affirmed their commitment to the social and economic vision of the union by recalling their engagement in the union's historic struggles for social justice. Many current programs in education, health care, and the arts affirmed the union's continued commitment to social unionism. One of my daughters now lives in cooperative housing developed by the ILGWU.

But as the business function of the union increased, its social justice activities diminished. The union became an integral part of the garment industry. It helped organize industrial boards that regulated prices and competition. It created its own engineering department to monitor piece rates. The research department provided reports and testimony before Congress to support legislation to restrict imports of lower priced garments. In regulating and reducing competition in the industry, the union tried to promote greater wage and employment stability. But the union's business function distanced the leadership from its membership.

On a sunny day in March 1958, I walked into the research department and was told we were walking down Broadway to Madison Square Garden to participate in a rally to support the Dress Makers Union's general strike. I donned my trench coat, turned up my collar, grabbed a strike sign, and marched with workers to the Broadway meeting. There had not been a general dress industry strike since 1933.

The rally began with Marc Starr, the union's educational director, encouraging everyone to join in singing "Solidarity Forever." I was seated among mostly Black and Hispanic women workers and soon realized they were singing the spiritual "Glory, Glory, Halleluiah" and not the union anthem. The union membership had changed, but the leadership had not. Hispanics and women of color, rather than Jews and Italians, now comprised the core of the membership. Aside from an aging Fania Cohen and Luigi Antonini, the leaders addressing the workers were mainly old white Jewish men.

I also learned that the strike was not only about wages and benefits. It had been called to deal with problems of non-union run-away shops that were undercutting the prices and work standards set in collective bargaining agreements. The strike also exposed a more troublesome problem: the increasing role of the mafia and criminal activity in the garment industry and the union. Leaders with criminal connections controlled the ILGWU's trucking local. When Dubinsky was asked, by a reporter, why the union didn't do more to purge those gangsters from the union's trucking local, he responded by asking the reporter whether he would like to volunteer for the job. It was a glib reply. I wondered whether a more democratic and socially mobilized union might have responded differently.

After the Madison Square Garden rally, I began thinking about resuming my studies at Columbia University. The research I did, while useful, was narrow in scope. Working for the ILGWU revealed the limited economic and political goals of trade unions, and I realized how wide the social and economic distance between the leadership and rank and file worker had become. Was this an inevitable paradox of the trade union's successful integration into the business system? Working for the union reopened questions about radical reform that had inspired my utopian dreams.

I decided to return to Columbia and devote more time to learning about alternative strategies and paths to economic and social reform. The decision had consequences, not only for me, but also for my wife and daughter Julie, who was born during this period. Time became a more precious resource. But of the many changes after returning to Columbia, none stands out more than our move to Manhattanville, a newly constructed public housing project for low-income families.

We moved into the first building located on Broadway and 126th Street. When completed, the project would encompass an area from Broadway and Amsterdam Avenues spanning from 126th Street to 133rd Street. The city had already built a large public housing project on the South side of 125th Street. While both had been built to replace the poor housing stock and offer improved housing for Western Harlem, we were told that the Manhattanville project would provide an integrated housing experience. It was an important reason why we decided to apply for an apartment. It also made it possible to live closer to the University.

I entered our building with great expectations. But after a long wait for one of the two elevators to take us up to the 19th floor, I wondered what might happen if one or both elevators broke down. But after seeing our newly completed two-bedroom apartment, I thought we had made the right decision.

That momentary confidence would soon fade as we settled into our new home.

My first project was building bookcases for the many books packed in boxes and stockpiled in our bedroom. I began drilling into the wall with a three-inch bit. What happened next startled me. I could see a light from the adjacent apartment coming from the hole I had drilled. Someone began banging on our door. I opened it to an angry Black woman shouting, "You're destroying our new apartment." It was the first of many incidents that revealed the poor quality of material used in constructing public housing for the poor and the potential social problems it created. Three inches of wall separated our bedroom from my Black neighbor's apartment. I learned to live with the noise and music that streamed through the walls of their apartment. I was fortunate. I enjoyed listening to the jazz their son played sometimes late into the night.

There were many reasons for our decision to look for another apartment in the neighborhood. During the four years we lived there, the elevators began to breakdown. Living on the 19th floor made this more than a passing inconvenience. More troublesome were signs of unsupervised teenagers and incidents of increased crime. It became evident that, in the not-too-distant future, a planned integrated public housing project would become segregated housing for the poor.

Working for the ILGWU and living in public housing changed how I managed my studies at Columbia University. More focused, I selected courses that I thought would enrich my understanding of the social and institutional underpinnings of economic change and development. I wanted to better understand what is but also what could be. How had economics been used to change the lives of ordinary people and what might be done differently? Columbia made those objectives difficult to implement. I recognized the important role my values played in channeling my intellectual interests. I was not fooled by economists who claimed their values did not influence their research. As the philosopher of science Morris Cohen observed, "Those who boast that they are as social scientists, not interested in what ought to be, generally assume (tacitly) the hitherto prevailing order is the proper ideal of what ought to be."

Seated at a long table in a small windowless room, I anxiously awaited the oral examination certifying my candidacy for the doctorate to begin. It had been a long journey with unexpected twists and turns—none more unnerving than what happened two weeks before the scheduled examination. Stunned, I listened in disbelief as the department secretary informed me that Professor A.R. Burns, an important member of my committee had been hospitalized and could not participate in the examination. She said I had a choice. I could cancel the orals or proceed as planned. Professor Michael

Florinsky had agreed to take on Professor Burns' responsibilities. "I advise you," she said, "not to make any hasty decisions before speaking to him."

I had spent almost a year studying the books and articles in an eight-page bibliography on comparative economic organization that Professor Burns had given me. He had provided no guidance on how to prepare for the examination. Nor was his textbook or his courses structured in a way that was helpful. I knew even less about Professor Florinsky's work. I was told he specialized in Russian and Soviet economic history. I thought it best that I see him.

He was talking on the phone when I entered his office. I noticed a large book entitled *The Encyclopedia of Russia and the Soviet Union,* which he had edited, prominently displayed in the center of his desk. What caught my eye changed what happened next. After a brief introduction I pointed to the volume and said, "I notice that my brother in-law, Earl Ubell, is one of the contributing editors of your book." Earl was at that time the science editor of the *New York Herald Tribune.*

Surprised, Florinsky said, "Earl is your brother in-law? What a wonderful man." He then began to speak about the book. I nodded and made some perfunctory comments about its importance. Finally, he glanced at a folder containing information about my pending examination and, with a smile, said, "Don't worry about the orals. Everything will be okay." Uncertain about what he meant, I asked if there was anything I should do in preparation. "No", he responded, "everything will be okay."

As the oldest member of my committee, Professor Florisnky chaired the examination. I had little problems answering most of the questions on economic theory posed by Professor Vickery or those by Professor Goran Ohlin on the economic history of Europe or by Professor Alexander Erlich on Soviet economic development. Professor Florinsky focused his questions on the Soviet Union, provoking a frustrated Professor Erlich to intervene, declaring, "Enough already, we know it was Stalin's fault." After the committee briefly deliberated, Professor Florinsky opened the door of the small seminar room and congratulated me. Elated, I thought how so much of life's journey is unpredictable.

The decision to choose Peronism as the subject of my Ph.D. dissertation was also fortuitous. My brother-in-law Ernesto Bravo, a leader in the Communist Party of Argentina, had been imprisoned and tortured by Peron and spent a year in the Soviet Union recovering from his wounds. After many conversations with Ernesto, I wondered how Peron had won the support of the working class. Was Peronism a movement of the left or the right? The mobilization of workers to serve a variety of political goals raised troubling questions about working-class authoritarianism. I went to Argentina to explore these questions.

Friends had recently posed similar questions about Donald Trump. Trump, like Peron, was a democratically elected president. Both developed movements that mobilized the support of workers. Peron organized them under the banner of "Argentina First." Trump used the slogan "America First." Both challenged liberal democratic principles. Peronism continues to be a powerful political movement in Argentina. Some argue that Trump is an American fascist. After months of research in Argentina I began to think of Peronism as a fascist movement of the left.

While I was marching in Buenos Aires with thousands of demonstrators demanding the inauguration of the duly elected Peronist delegates to the Parliament, soldiers suddenly began firing at the crowd. Everyone scrambled for safety. I ducked into a small street, astonished that many of the demonstrators were laughing. Did they know something I didn't? Matters suddenly seemed more menacing when tanks appeared, spraying indelible red dye into the crowd in order to more easily tag those who had participated in the protest. What I witnessed in 1962 confirmed my sense that the end of Peron's Presidency was just the beginning of a movement that had planted deep roots in Argentine politics and society.

He began building his legacy as defender of the working class when he was appointed Secretary of Labor after a military coup in 1943. He began using his position to secure the support of workers and their unions. But unlike Trump, who reached out to those forgotten industrial workers displaced by technology and foreign competition, Peron's strongest source of support came from rural migrant workers seeking opportunities within an expanding industrial working class.

Trump arose to power proclaiming that he would bring back a "glorious" time in America when affluent and secure industrial workers were connected to American culture and society. He offered America's white workers a means to vent their frustrations about their loss of dignity and power, but offered no viable path to a better future. Rather than empowering workers, Trump used their discontent to ferment racist and anti-immigrant sentiments around his promise to "Make America Great Again." He used his support among a divided working class to ignite a proto-fascist populist movement of the right.

Peron came to power under different social and economic circumstances. He challenged the landed elite who dominated an agricultural economy dependent on foreign trade especially with Great Britain. Seeking to develop its industry, Peron mobilized the support of workers and their unions as well as corporations for his vision of a new independent industrial Argentina. In doing so he threatened established elites. While he controlled the media and the military and used authoritarian methods to repress opposition, he remained vulnerable to the landed elites, the church, and some officers in the military who were critical of his polices. But Peron's success posed difficult questions for socialists and communists; it raised doubts about the worker's role in the march toward socialism.

In a seminar at Columbia the labor economist Aaron Warner claimed that Marxists predicted that workers would, in response to the ills of capitalism, develop a revolution consciousness and become its gravediggers. Rather delicately, I responded that Marxists believed that, left to their own means, workers would develop a more limited trade union consciousness. It would take a political movement to cultivate socialist solutions to their problems. To my surprise Professor Warner turned to a student and said, "Let's ask Mr. Ismyloff, who is a member of the Soviet delegation to United Nations what he thinks."

With some reluctance Ismyloff replied, "I'm afraid I must agree with Mr. Silverman."

In Argentina the communists were not the only political party competing for the allegiance of the working class. Peron revealed that fascists could successfully command working-class support. Rejecting liberal capitalism *and* socialism, Peron created a political movement that rested on three ideological goals: social justice for workers, economic independence, and political sovereignty. He sought to enlist workers and an emerging industrial capitalist class in constructing a modern economy no longer dependent on Great Britain and other more-developed economies. The key to his political ambitions rested on the support of the working class.

During his revolutionary phase Peron, with his wife Eva, did improve the lives of workers. With his support, the size and power of trade unions increased dramatically, their leadership increasingly under his control. He nationalized some key industries and organized industrial companies into corporate associations to bargain collectively with trade unions. By the end of 1949 Peron had developed an ambitious welfare state that dwarfed Roosevelt's New Deal; he had created a fascism of the left.

Peron recruited labor activists to serve as labor attaches to implant Peronist ideology throughout Latin America. In doing so, he competed with a rival group of labor attachés working closely with the United States government, the CIA, and large corporations in efforts to contain communism. I met one of those labor attachés at the American embassy in Buenos Aires. He confirmed my suspicions that the CIA closely monitored trade union activities and radical politics in Argentina.

It was a fortuitous encounter. I discovered that Martin had worked for the ILGWU. Whatever reservations he might have had in sharing information with me softened as we recounted our ILGWU experiences. I was somewhat surprised that he seemed more troubled by potential communist influence in Argentine trade unions than with the Peronist controlled unions. But I should not have been surprised. I knew that his boss, Jay Lovestone, the Director of International Affairs for the ILGWU, worked for the CIA and the U.S. State Department to help monitor communist influence in trade unions.

Martin offered little insight into Peronism. Still, I thought I was beginning to unravel some of the contradictions of left fascism. Peron believed he could use the power of the State to sharply increase the income of the working class and transform Argentina from a dependent agricultural economy to an independent developed industrial society. He won the support of the working class but failed to create an economically independent Argentina. If Sweden represented efforts by social democrats to find a middle ground between capitalism and communism, Peronism is an example of a neo-fascist movement seeking to occupy the same political space. Sweden became a successful social democratic nation. Peronism was politically successful but an economic failure.

Peron could boast that, during his presidency, workers increased their share of national income from about 40 percent to about 60 percent of national income. But Argentine economic growth was a dismal failure. Per capita income barely grew during Peron's presidency. As the income of workers exceeded worker productivity and inflation eroded real income, his goals of economic independence and political sovereignty faded. He then turned to political repression to contain political dissent, but he could not sustain the support of the Argentinian elites. A military coup ended his presidency but did not end working-class faith in Peronism.

Many workers still believe in Peron's promise of an independent and just Argentina.

Despite their limited role in Argentine politics, communists had their own utopian dreams. The Cuban Revolution had rekindled visions of a new socialist future. My brother-in-law Ernesto introduced me to some of his communist friends at a time when both the Peronist and Communist parties had been banned. The communists I met were unlike those I had known during the McCarthy period in New York City. They were more militant and defiant yet more privileged. Many carried guns and lived in large apartments and gated houses. Servants cared for their children and did the housework. More secure about their place in society, they seemed less preoccupied with consumerism and their economic status than their American counterparts. At one of their informal dinners, I met Che Guevara's sister. Dressed fashionably and wearing high leather boots, she, like her friends, was a committed communist.

While the conversation focused on the political situation in Argentina, they also voiced concerns about potential problems in Cuba and the threat of a United States invasion. Cuba had turned to the Soviet Union for political and economic support as conflicts with the United States sharpened. Some wondered what effect that would have on the Cuban Revolution, hoping that Cuba would find its own path to socialism. I did not know then that I would soon travel to Cuba to explore its utopian road to socialism.

Chapter 5

DREAMS AND ILLUSIONS

HAVE OFTEN WONDERED WHY it is the young and not their elders who ignite movements for radical change. Is it Eros, so strongly evident in our youth, that powers movements seeking to transform our way of living? The Nobel laureate Bob Dylan captured such a moment when he warned that the young were beyond our command and sweeping changes were taking place.

The winds of change surfaced as the decade of the 1960s opened and a younger generation began questioning the consumerist and self-indulgent concerns of their parents' generation. I returned from Argentina in 1962 to face these changes. The grievances of the young were not just about the hypocrisy of proclaimed beliefs in freedom and the reality of black oppression. They also challenged a consumer culture that undermined civic engagement and promoted false promises of an affluent utopia. I began to wonder whether my slogan "want less, get more" was taking root. Visions of a post materialist society were blossoming, my utopian dreams awakening.

And yet for many prominent intellectuals the political protests of the 1960s were unforeseen. Daniel Bell's book *The End of Ideology* could not have come at a worse moment. Published in 1960 just as the Civil Rights Movement found its voice, he and his collaborators argued that fundamental disagreements among political adversaries had declined sharply. Welfare State capitalism in the West had found a way of resolving social and economic conflicts. The old battles envisioned by Marxists and socialists, he proclaimed, were over, visions of a utopian future no longer relevant.

But there were voices on the right as well as those on the left who challenged Bell's thesis that the old ideological battles were over. I remember reading disapproving remarks that Frederick Hayek made during a World Congress of Intellectuals held in Italy in 1955. Evidently outraged by assertions that the ideological battles between the left and the right had ended, he insisted that socialism still posed an existential threat to freedom. Most of the participants at the conference dismissed his concerns. Twenty years later Hayek would win the Noble Prize in economics and lead an effective neo-liberal crusade against the welfare state.

In the summer of 1962, it seemed as if the times were indeed changing. I began teaching at Cooper Union for the Advancement of Art and Sciences and sensed the shifting temperament of my students, especially those majoring in architecture. One incident was emblematic of those times. As I casually entered a classroom prepared to begin a discussion about current social and economic problems, I discovered to my surprise an empty classroom. I looked at the blackboard and saw a note written in bold letters: *Out To Demonstrate With C.O.R.E.* I was about to leave when one of my students entered the room. In a firm voice I told him to go to the office and bring back the blue books we use for examinations. He looked puzzled. I told him I thought the other students would soon return. Ten minutes later they entered, smiling, while I looked at them disapprovingly.

When they were seated, I began distributing the blue books as I said, "I know you think this is funny, but I think it's an example of bad behavior that suggests you're not doing the reading assignments for the course. This exam will tell me if that's true or not. And by the way, I have decided that this test will determine 50 percent of your final grade. I know some of you expect to graduate this year. Let's hope your grade on this test does not prevent that from happening." I then turned to the blackboard and began writing the questions for the quiz. I heard students whispering, "Is he really going to do this?"

"No," one whispered, "he's kidding."

When I completed the first question and started on the second, a student yelled, "Oh, my God, he's serious."

At that moment I turned, smiling, and said, "OK. You have just experienced a clear example of the abuse of power."

A student stood up, clearly agitated, and yelled, "But we would have taken care of you one evening when you weren't looking."

"Well," I said, smiling. "You just learned an important lesson about the uses of power. Power corrupts, but powerlessness also corrupts."

In the next few years, a resurgent radicalism ignited a new left politics. Utopia entered the political discourse. In a prescient article, the sociologist C. Wright Mills asserted, "What needs to be understood, and what needs to be changed, is not merely first this and then that detail of some institution or policy. If there is to be a politics of a New Left, what needs to be analyzed is the structure of institutions, the foundation of politics. In this sense, both in its criticism and in its proposals, our work is necessarily structural— and just now—Utopian."

Renewed political activism promoted visions of new possibilities. The 1963 March on Washington that took place on my birthday suggested that the consumerist culture of the 1950s might be ebbing and engagement in radical politics rising. The personal took on a political dimension as well. To change the culture and society, some intellectuals and more advantaged white students explored new ways of living. Many turned to Freud and Marx for answers.

While inspired by the revival of political engagement, I wondered whether some aspects of Mills' necessary utopia might distract rather than further the new left's radical agenda. The Civil Rights Movement from which the New Left had sprung offered a more focused political strategy than those advocated by more affluent white students seeking to radically change their personal lives. Yet I soon realized that the personal was intimately connected to the politics of the time.

An emerging women's movement interrogated how structures of power built on gender and sexuality were embedded in family and personal relations. The slogan "the personal is political" suggested how deeply hierarchical constructs were entrenched in our consciousness and belief systems. And the peace and anti-war movements exposed the threat the Vietnam War posed to our very existence. But some demanded more. The counterculture challenged norms central to the workings of a capitalist society. In their dress, the use of drugs, and sexual behavior they sought different ways of living. Some created alternative utopian communities. I didn't think this was the utopian strategy Mills had in mind. I became increasingly troubled that many young radicals had not sufficiently evaluated the resistance they faced in their efforts to transform American capitalism.

Two books that my students read exposed how structures of power dominated every aspect of our lives. The philosopher Herbert Marcuse, drawing on Freud and Marx, painted a daunting picture of advanced industrial societies' subversion of critical thought and action. In his book *One-Dimensional Man,* Marcuse argued that contemporary capitalism had effectively integrated people into established systems of production and consumption. The media, advertising industry, and the management of labor fashioned an affluent society that limited possibilities and opportunities for radical change. His concept of repressive de-sublimation suggested that greater sexual freedom, rather than contributing to human flourishing, diminished creativity by exploiting the sexual and loving dimensions of human interactions. Marcuse put it this way: "The people recognize themselves in their commodities; they find their soul in their automobile, hi-fi set, split level home, kitchen equipment." These false needs that capitalism had created were a form of control that perpetuated the "toil, misery, and injustice" of capitalism.

Marcuse's critique of capitalism's effective management of behavior and consciousness inspired rather than deterred the New Left. In contrast to traditional Marxists, Marcuse questioned the revolutionary role of the working class and the inevitability of capitalist crisis. The source of radical change, he argued, would come from minorities, outsiders, and radical intellectuals who promoted critical thinking and radical opposition to the existing order. Many young radicals and intellectuals heard his call to arms as they took to the streets. I wondered whether they understood the enormous obstacles they faced.

One encounter I witnessed suggested that some students had not fully grasped Marcuse's message. Listening to a lecture while attending a Socialist Scholars Conference at Columbia University, I noticed a group of undergraduates seated behind me smoking marijuana. Halfway into the lecture they became abusive, shouting, "Shut up, enough already, fuck you." I turned to see who was disrupting the speaker. To my surprise it was Marc Rudd, a leader of Columbia's SDS. Suddenly a voice in the back of the auditorium shouted, "Enough." I turned as an older gray-haired man rose to speak. "This is an outrage!" he exclaimed. "You are violating the principles of democratic participation—and on the anniversary of the Paris Commune." I wonder if Marc Rudd knew that the man admonishing him was Herbert Marcuse.

Two prominent Marxist economists, Paul Sweezy and Paul Baran, were also rethinking how affluent capitalist society's function. Sweezy was for many the dean of American Marxist economists, his magazine *Monthly Review* an important source of Marxist analysis of current economic and political trends. Sweezy and Baran's book *Monopoly Capitalism* maintained that the central problem capitalists faced was not creating the surplus value needed for investment but rather finding ways of reinvesting an expanding economic surplus to avoid economic crisis and stagnation.

The utopian possibilities Keynes envisioned at this stage of capitalist development contrasted sharply with the one projected by Sweezy and Baran. They painted a picture of an economy that misused its resources, increased economic inequality, and created a debased consumerist culture. They exposed how large corporations and the government, rather than ending the money motive and sharply reducing working time as Keynes had predicted, instead spent the growing economic surplus. Since corporations resisted raising the wages and social benefits of workers, the surplus was invested in lavish spending by the rich, and on advertising, sales promotion, excessive product changes, and military and defense appropriations that promoted endless wars. Financial trading and speculation increased sharply as corporations and the wealthy sought new ways of investing their wealth but at the risk of greater debt and financial instability.

Strikingly missing from this depressing picture was a discussion of the working class, the gravediggers of capitalism in Marx's analysis. Was this a consequence of capitalism's successes rather than its failures? If so, who would replace the worker as the radical agents of change? Sweezy and Baran, like Marcuse, looked outside our borders to countries on the periphery seeking independence from foreign control as sources for radical change. For many on the left, Cuba had become a symbol of revolutionary possibilities. At the end of 1967 I began thinking about studying Cubans' new path to socialism.

Thoughts about traveling to Cuba came at a moment when students and civil rights protests awakened demands for radical change. Events in April 1968 unfolded rapidly, sparking demonstrations against the Vietnam War and racial injustice. In the Fall of 1967, I finally completed my Ph.D. and began teaching at Hofstra University. I frequently drove from Hempstead, Long Island, to Manhattan with colleagues from the Economics Department. As I passed over the Tri-Borough Bridge the evening on April 4, 1968, I had an uneasy feeling I might encounter some problems.

It was the day Martin Luther King was assassinated. My car slowly moved across West 126th Street, approaching a traffic light at end of the block. I could see a large group of Black youth standing near the intersection, yelling and smashing windows as cars stopped for the light. Inching up to the intersection I wondered if shouting, "Hey, we're the good guys!" would mean anything. Fortunately, the light changed as I approached, and I evaded the enraged group venting its anger over the murder of a visionary leader in the struggle for social justice.

Toward the end of April, a strike by Columbia students exposed the volatility of the political climate. Protests at the University of California at Berkeley and the University of Michigan had already taken place. But what happened at Columbia University ignited one of the largest student protests in United States history. Sparked by the planned construction of a university gymnasium in nearby Morningside Park and the exposure of faculty research supporting the Vietnam War, students occupied Hamilton Hall, the main building of the college.

As an alumnus, I frequently came to the campus to support the students. While the two groups that led the strike, Students for a Democratic Society and The Student Afro Society, had different priorities and objectives, those divisions ended as I witnessed police beating and arresting students injuring many. During that politically charged moment, I finalized my plans to travel to Cuba. It would be a life-changing experience but not in the way I had imagined.

Cuba had been on my mind. The Cuban revolution had sparked admiration among New Left radicals. For many young activists, Fidel Castro and Che Guevara symbolized the potential of revolutionary action. I wondered whether Peron's "left fascism" and Fidel's "revolutionary socialism" shared some common roots. The strength of both social movements depended on the political support and mobilization of ordinary workers. But unlike Peronism, a small band of Cuban revolutionaries had overthrown the existing social order. Social, political, and economic power structures crumbled and needed to be rebuilt. Almost ten years had passed since that historic moment. Was Cuba's path to socialism different from the road taken by the Soviet Union and other socialist countries? I decided to see for myself.

I was especially drawn to Che's vision that "to build communism a new man must be created simultaneously with the material base." Economic and social development must depend on moral rather than material incentives. Yet I was troubled by aspects of Che's audacity. For him, "the true revolutionary is guided by strong feelings of love. . . . Our vanguard revolutionaries must idealize their love for the people. . . . There is no life outside the revolution."

Karl Marx famously suggested that some historic moments are farcical and at times even absurd. There were moments during my time in Cuba when I thought farce was a fitting epitaph to what I was witnessing. And yet what I observed had elements of tragedy. I described it this way. "The scenario is all there: The heroic figures of Che and Fidel engulfed in a noble and uplifting purpose, and yet confronting complex social forces which divert their intentions. Che's fate is known. But the struggle between revolutionary will and the power of circumstances is an ongoing dialectic of the Cuban revolution."

But I'm getting ahead of my story.

My trip to Cuba posed some special challenges. I traveled with my wife and two children, Julie and Devi. I also invited my brother and sister-in-law, Ann and Marvin Leiner, and their three children, Kenny, Karen, and Danny, to join us.

My sister-in-law Estella and her husband Ernesto, and their three children, then living in Cuba helped us apply for the necessary invitations and visas from the Cuban government that made travel to Cuba possible. Families can be nurturing but also a source of tension and stress. My first inkling of potential problems occurred during the planning stage of our trip.

Two incidents should have raised some red flags. The first came from a surprise message from Estella informing me that Marvin had written to her about his Cuban plans. I asked him why he had written such a letter without mentioning that I had initiated the idea and had invited him to join us. Embarrassed, he responded defensively, suggesting that he was only exploring the idea. His explanation was not reassuring.

The second incident was more troublesome. Going to Cuba required outside funding. Since I had recently completed a study of Peronism, I thought I would be the one most likely to find financial support. So I told Marvin I would share whatever funds I received and suggested we pool our financial resources so that no one would be left behind. He happily agreed. As the months passed, I wondered whether either of us would find the necessary financial aid. I was therefore encouraged when I discovered that the Ford Foundation might be interested in my project. I immediately told Marvin the news. He looked at me sheepishly. "I know. I met with people at Ford Foundation, and they're willing to fund my project." I was angry but also deeply hurt. It was a harbinger of things to come. In the end we were both awarded Ford Foundation grants that would ironically limit the resources I could mobilize to conduct my Cuban research.

In addition to Ernesto and Estella's assistance, a friendship with Ricardo Alarcon, the Cuban ambassador to the United Nations, also helped facilitate travel to Cuba. Our bond was cemented on a summer day in July a few months before leaving for Cuba. I had invited Ricardo and his wife and young daughter to Great Neck, Long Island, to spend the day and evening with our family. That summer we were temporarily living in my brother-in-law's house, with access to a private swimming pool and play area for the children. Ricardo needed special permission to come Great Neck because it was beyond the thirty-mile radius he was permitted to travel.

Everything proceeded without incident. We spent the afternoon lounging by the pool and relaxing in the living room, talking about their life in New York, when the phone rang. It was a neighbor asking anxiously, "What's going on in your house? There are police everywhere."

I put down the phone and went to the window. There were at least five police cars with lights flashing and many neighbors mulling around. I turned to Ricardo and said, "I think we might have visitors."

Suddenly the garden door burst open and two high-booted and armed state troopers entered the living room. Shocked, I shouted, "What's going on?"

One of the officers asked, "Is the ambassador from the Dominican Republic here?"

"No," I said, "only the Cuban ambassador to the United Nations. You have no right barging into our house and need to leave immediately." I looked at them defiantly, waiting for their response. To my surprise they simply turned and left. I believe my encounter with police that day may have helped expedite obtaining the visas we needed for travel to Cuba.

Preparing for our stay in Cuba produced other conflicts and tensions. Besides subletting our Manhattanville apartment, we needed to shop for a large variety of items that Estella wanted and thought our family would need. I was especially alarmed when she suggested we ship our car as well. We bought two large trunks and filled them with clothing, linens, towels, toiletries, vitamins, medical supplies, and many other products. I began to wonder whether life in revolutionary Cuba might be quite different than I imagined.

Some initial experiences in Cuba also raised some concerns.

Looking out on the city from the balcony of the Havana Libre, I felt like a tourist separated from the lives of ordinary Cubans. I should have been more grateful, but this was not the Cuba I had come to see. Our apartment had a very large living room and two bedrooms, each with its own bathroom and balcony. All the services of the hotel were freely available, as well as a car and a driver. The next day Estella and her family arrived for lunch served by the hotel staff. It was a joyful reunion. I felt a little churlish when I asked Estie (her family name) how long it would take before we could begin to lead more normal lives. A month would pass before our families moved into apartments one block from where the Bravos lived.

Our large three-bedroom apartment had been previously owned by affluent Cubans then living in the United States. With Estie's, help we hired a full-time housekeeper who did most of the housework and, when necessary, cared for our children. Georgina soon became part of our family. She lived among other poor Cubans in a small one-room, corrugated tin-like structure without running water along the side of our apartment building. I felt as if we were living no differently than the middle-class Argentinians I had met in Buenos Aires. That mindset soon faded as our daily life in Cuba unfolded and I began to appreciate the formidable challenges Cuba faced.

"The Year of the Revolutionary Offensive" was the name the Cuban leadership bestowed on the time I spent in Cuba. It marked a radical shift in Cuba's road to socialism. When I arrived, Ernesto asked what I planned to study while in Cuba. I told him I was interested in exploring the use of moral rather than material incentives in Cuba's efforts to transform its economy. His reaction troubled me. "Bert, that's a complicated issue. You might consider studying something else."

On September 28, 1968, a few weeks after we arrived, I sat on a stage in the Plaza de La Revolucion with other Cuban leaders and government officials, waiting for Fidel Castro to begin his speech commemorating the eighth anniversary of the Committees for the Defense of the Revolution. These neighborhood organizations had been formed to engage the Cuban people in community activities and to help identify anti-social or subversive behavior. Watching the more than a quarter of a million people from Havana and the surrounding provinces, I listened to their thunderous shouts: "Fidel, Fidel!"

As his speech unfolded it became evident that Fidel's economic plans would radically change how Cubans worked and lived. I had never witnessed such a performance. For almost five hours the charismatic leader of the revolution used his speech to inspire and inform the Cuban people and its leaders about a new path the revolution had taken and what needed to be done to overcome skepticism and resistance. I soon realized why Ernesto was troubled about my planned research. The subject of moral incentives touched a central theme of Fidel's speech.

Fidel proclaimed that the Revolutionary Offensive marked the beginning of a real revolution. His called for nothing less than a change of the nation's soul. "Let us not mistake the triumph of sentiment, the triumph of enthusiasm, the triumph of emotions for the triumph of consciousness." He reminded the workers of Havana's gaudy and vulgar past: its social and economic inequality, bureaucracy, commerce, gambling, speculative activities, and the privileges of the petty bourgeois and labor aristocracy. But he exclaimed that the revolution had changed all this. In a booming voice he proclaimed, "It took years for the triumph of revolutionary consciousness to reach our masses, but in the last year we truly believe that this revolutionary consciousness has become apparent in the masses of our capital." At that moment I appreciated the importance of moral incentives in Cuba's socialist revolution. But I also knew that ideological pronouncements could not by themselves change behavior; that would depend on people's actual experiences.

I listened as Fidel launched into a detailed description of efforts to develop a green belt around Havana. I would learn about other major initiatives that sounded promising but were never realized. Cuban leaders seated near me were taking notes as if learning about many of these plans for the first time. At some point the tone of the speech shifted as Fidel began to launch an attack on his critics. "Those who never believe in anything and saw everything as impossible, a fantasy—first the ten-million-ton sugar plan, but also other plans. What they did not see was the will and efforts of a revolutionary people." But he also acknowledged the shortages of goods and services that hampered production and undermined living conditions and the struggles against counter-revolutionary behavior.

And then he warned, "Every *gusano* [worm] should know. This is a struggle for the survival of the revolution where half-measures are ruled out. The action we take must be extreme." Was coercion also a necessary part of the Revolutionary Offensive? Fidel began to cite examples of anti-social behavior among young people in Havana and asked if they wanted to introduce a version of Prague into Cuba. Many in the audience knew he was referring to the Soviet suppression of the Czechoslovakian rebellion earlier in the year. Fidel acknowledged that young people faced many problems including insufficient secondary schools. To engage them in productive work, he revealed that the military had created youth brigades, citing the activities of the Centennial Youth Column in Camaguey Providence, and the part they were playing in the sugar harvest.

After devoting so much of his speech to the commitments workers needed to make in fulfilling the goals of the revolution, Fidel began to envision a future when machines would ease the toil of the Cuban worker, a time when work would no longer be burdensome and consume so much of the worker's time. Was Fidel using this utopian dream to deflect current reality? He ended his speech with a warning: "Liberalism, no; softening, no; a revolutionary people, an organized people, a combative people, these are the virtues that are needed in these years. All the rest is pure illusion." As I listened to these words, I wondered what was possible and what was illusory in Fidel's revolutionary offensive.

During the Year of the Revolutionary Offensive the state took control of the remaining private sector. The government nationalized large and middle-sized businesses. Small businesses were closed, shutting down the bodegas, barbershops, shoe and auto repair shops, restaurants, small bars, and many other tiny establishments that had played important roles in the social and economic life of the Cuban people. Almost all food was rationed. Small farms of less than 165 acres were the only legal private enterprises remaining. They became an important source of income for farmers who sold their surplus products on the black market. Most Cubans were forced to find other means of obtaining those lost services. It didn't take long before I realized why Fidel spoke about creating a "new man" motivated by revolutionary consciousness rather than economic self-interest.

In the beginning my research consisted of visits arranged by Cuban officials to a few innovative ventures and experiments in farming and industry. I knew that these showcase projects were not the real face of the Cuban economy. I began exploring Havana and the surrounding area on my own. These forays provided a glimpse into the lives of ordinary Cubans. They exposed the shortages of food and consumer services, but they also revealed the availability of free schooling, medical care, transportation, recreational facilities, and low-cost housing. Although many of those services were not always easily accessible or of the highest quality, they existed.

I don't remember exactly when my misgivings about Cuba's radical economic agenda began. I was drawn to the nation's vision of creating a new path to socialism. I tried to see what was happening through Cuba's perspective. I recognized the obstacles it faced as it sought to implement its revolutionary economic policies. The Bay of Pigs, the blockade of Cuban trade, and other efforts by the United States to undermine the Cuban revolution understandably increased the leadership's sensitivity to criticism of the revolution.

I remember my own efforts to encourage greater objectivity among my Cooper Union students when the Cuban missile crisis unfolded in 1962. During those terrifying moments I asked them whether they agreed or disagreed with the President's statement that our country could never tolerate nuclear missiles ninety miles from our shore. When they nodded in agreement, I asked whether they would still agree with that statement if the president who issued that proclamation was Fidel Castro.

But the Cuban leaders demanded more. Allowable criticism of the revolution was encapsulated in the slogan, "Everything within the Revolution and nothing outside it—" a warning that would significantly limit what I would be able to do, especially after an Argentine newspaper raised troubling questions about the Ford Foundation's support of my research. The article accused the Ford Foundation of seeking to undermine radical reform in Latin America. Suddenly, promised support for my research ended. Appointments for meetings were broken. I soon realized that what I could do would depend primarily on personal observations, interviews with Cuban leaders, visits to factories and farms, and available articles and reports.

In reviewing Cuban journals, I discovered a moment when Cuban leaders openly confronted some fundamental questions facing Cuban socialism. During the first few years after taking power, the government mobilized popular support by radically redistributing income and by igniting nationalist sentiments against threats of military intervention by United State. It was a moment when improvements in living standards were fortified by rapid economic growth. Some Cuban economic planners predicted that, in ten years, Cubans would have the same living standards as West Europeans. But instead of increasing, Cuban living standards began to decline. During this period Cuban leaders and foreign advisors began to consider alternative ways of organizing the economy. Out of this controversy the Great Debate about alternative paths to socialism was born.

The debate intrigued me. The controversy focused on how best to organize and plan the Cuban economy. The participants included members of the Council of Ministers and some well- known European Marxist economists. The debate began as a response to critics who blamed Cuba's reliance on centralized economic planning, rather than on market pricing and decentralized decision-making, for Cuba's economic problems. I thought I had uncovered a controversy not unlike the Great Industrialization Debates in the Soviet Union.

As Minister of Industry Che Guevara had moved rapidly to control the management of individual firms. Che believed that central supervision of individual firms was necessary because many experienced managers, financial officers, and accountants had left the country and could not easily be replaced. Recently hired and inexperienced managers, while committed to the revolution, needed to follow the directives of planners who coordinated industrial production. Che turned to a system of centralized budgeting rather than market prices to control and guide managerial decisions. Nor were material incentives useful at a time when consumer goods were rationed and real income declining. For Che moral incentives provided the only consistent path for creating an economy built on socialist values.

An alternative, more decentralized, economic system of self-finance also existed at this time. It was officially sanctioned by the Director of Agriculture, Carlos Raphael Rodriguez, and the Foreign

Trade Minister, Alberto Mora. In the system of self-finance, firms were legally independent and exchanged their products through markets. Their success was determined by their profitability. Managers relied on market prices and material incentives in guiding their decisions. Although firms had considerable financial independence, each had to cover their current expenses. Banks provided the funds needed to run their businesses and played a critical role in evaluating and controlling their performance.

In reviewing the debate, I was struck by Che's faith in the revolution's capacity to anticipate "the steps to be taken to force the pace of events." He defended the importance of human volition in radically transforming the Cuban economy. "Why think that the setbacks dealt by reality to certain bold acts stem exclusively from boldness rather than—perhaps entirely— from technical deficiency in administration?" But Alberto Mora's offered a prescient warning. He cautioned that economic institutions should be structured in ways that would "prevent the substitution of the money motive for the power motive." Would a belief in the revolution's ability to rapidly create a socialist economy undermine the development of democratic institutions?

At first Fidel expressed impatience with the debate. "Our obligation," he exclaimed, "is not only to theorize in the field of philosophy." But when I arrived in Cuba in the Fall of 1968, Fidel began advocating a radical version of Che's ideas embracing an economy based only on moral incentives. The debate had clearly ended. Fidel warned that many would be critical of Cuba's decisions, but he claimed that the "facts will speak for us, and realities will speak for us." I would soon discover how difficult it would be for those closest to me to accept the facts and realities of Cuba's chosen revolutionary path to socialism.

In the months that followed I visited factories and farms and interviewed Cuban officials, managers of enterprises, and trade union leaders. It soon became apparent that every aspect of economic and social life had been touched by Cuba's ambitious economic goals. Trade union meetings focused on labor discipline and the mobilization of volunteer workers. But exhortations and appeals to revolutionary commitment could not compensate for shortages of raw materials and spare parts necessary to sustain worker productivity. In many factories workers willing to work overtime stood by their bunk beds with nothing to do. The planning system could not be depended on to coordinate economic activity. Under such conditions neither moral nor material incentives were effective motivational tools. A troubling picture began to emerge. Not only the mobilization of voluntary labor but the use of military had become increasingly necessary to fulfill Cuba's economic goals.

I was distressed by the dismissive criticism I encountered from my family as I began voicing my apprehensions about the troubling realities of Cuba's Revolutionary Offensive. "You don't understand what Cuba's is trying to do. Why are you always so critical? Why do think you know more than Fidel or Che?" I had hoped my family would be understanding and caring. Instead, they seemed dismissive and detached. I turned to Evie for support. But she was torn by loyalty to her sister and to the Cuban revolution, and unable to understand what I was experiencing. Disturbing feelings of loneliness and anxiety began to affect my sense of purpose. My youthful dreams started to fade. I thought I might need professional help. I hesitated, concerned that seeing a therapist might somehow undermine my research. I finally turned to Ernesto and asked if he knew someone in the medical school I could see.

I soon began a rather unusual therapy. My psychiatrist, Eduardo, was not fluent in English, and I was not always certain whether my Spanish adequately captured all that I was feeling. I also worried about the confidentiality of the therapy. But as our sessions unfolded, those concerns gradually faded. Eduardo encouraged me to speak openly about my experiences and observations of Cuban social and economic policies. Astonished by my accounts of interviews with Cuban leaders, he often began our session by asking, "So, Bert, who have you spoken to this week?" Sharing many of my experiences with Eduardo eased my anxiety and restored my self-confidence.

A conversation with the Secretary of Labor, Commandante Jorge Risquet, provided some important insights into the social and economic factors that determined Cuba's dependence on moral rather than material incentives. Dressed in olive green fatigues, he greeted me warmly. His military rank and credentials underscored the important role he had played in Cuba's revolution. He had recently returned from Angola, where along with Che he led Cuba's military taskforce. Unlike Ricardo Alarcon, he had been an active member of the Cuba's communist party since his teenage years.

Open, direct, and confident, Risquet defended Cuba's reliance on moral incentives as a logical response to the economic challenges Cuba faced. Unlike Che, he didn't refer to the goal of creating a "new socialist man." Instead, he argued that Cuba could not rely on material incentives when workers were asked to work more and consume less. Under such conditions material incentives would merely heighten feelings of economic sacrifice. Only incentives promoting worker's collective efforts toward common goals were politically and economically viable. "How can Cuba emphasize material incentives at a time of serious shortages and economic sacrifices, when ninety miles away such goals can be more easily fulfilled? We would simply create conditions for the mass migration of Cubans to the United States."

I was tempted to ask whether material incentives could be repressed at a time when marginal economic differences in economic conditions were magnified. But as our conversation unfolded, it became evident that Cuba's goal of producing an unprecedented ten million tons of sugar required extensive use of unpaid voluntary labor and the redeployment of workers from more skilled to less skilled and menial work. And most ominously, Cuba's economic plans required substantial increases in capital investments. To find the savings necessary to fund those investments, the leadership had little choice but to call on the Cuban people to consume less at a time when living standards were declining. But additional cutbacks in consumption were undermining worker productivity. It appeared that a primary source for funding Cuba's ambitious economic plan could only come from workers' unpaid labor. Was Cuba embarking on the path of primitive accumulation, where force would be necessary to generate the resources needed for economic development?

I looked at Eduardo, wondering how much more I should say. But he anticipated my concerns. "Not all Cubans are revolutionaries," he said, "and they have many other pressing concerns and priorities."

"Yes," I said. "Moral incentives, if they are truly individually motivated, cannot be imposed from above. How can you plan voluntary work? Isn't that a contradiction in terms? Would force we necessary?" Eduardo nodded. I smiled. Finally, there was a place where I could be heard.

Dismissively, Estie shouted, "Don't you understand? Cuba is creating a new society where money no longer matters." "Look", she said, as she cut a twenty-peso note in half.

I shook my head in disbelief. "You've only demonstrated that the peso has lost its value and why Cubans are turning to barter to get what they need. That's not socialism. As the peso loses its purchasing power, Cuba will have to depend on extracting more labor from Cuban workers to achieve the economic objectives of the revolution. And that's very difficult to plan or organize."

Shaking her head Estie responded dismissively, "You need to have more faith in revolution."

What did 'faith in the revolution' mean? Toward the end of our time in Cuba, Estie was able to get permission for our family to shop at the diplomatic store. Most Cubans purchased their food in government-run bodegas. Visits to those stores revealed how restricted the Cuban diet had become and why barter and access to the remaining private agricultural market had become increasingly important. A black market existed where stolen and illegally obtained goods could be bought at some risk. We shopped at a place reserved for foreign technicians. But even that store had little inventory and a limited variety of food products. I discovered how aggressive Soviet and East European women could be when competing for those scarce products, often wondering whether they had honed those skills in their home countries. Shopping at the diplomats' dollar store provided access to products I had not seen since coming to Cuba. For the first time in eight months, we could buy cheese, butter, ham, fruit, and ice cream. Whatever guilt Estie might have felt quickly faded as she took advantage of our new privileges.

Cuba's *ad hoc* efforts to deal with shortages of basic consumer goods were at times impulsive. The campaign to increase the consumption of rabbit meat was such an example. Since rabbits reproduced quickly, Fidel believed that, by encouraging the consumption of rabbits, Cuba could reduce its reliance on pork and other more expensive meat products. To change Cuban's dietary habits, he proposed opening rabbit restaurants throughout Cuba.

I decided to make a reservation for six at the first rabbit restaurant to open in Havana. The restaurant boasted of serving thirty varieties of rabbit dishes. The relatively high prices did not deter many Cubans, who were awash in unspent pesos. I would spend two full days and nights on a line waiting to make a reservation for our family. I learned a great deal while standing on that queue, especially the difference between *socioismo* and *socialismo*, a distinction many "revolutionary tourists" failed to make.

The friendliness and generosity of Cubans I encountered made waiting on the queue for those many hours less burdensome. Perhaps naively, I began wondering whether some attributes of Cuban culture already existed on which a more cooperative society could be built. Soon after I joined the line, I learned that a committee had been formed to prevent cheating and find ways to help families organize the time they spent queuing up. I never saw anyone violate the rules that were established.

We ate very well that Sunday afternoon. I had never eaten rabbit. While it was not part of their diet, Cubans ordered more than they could possibly eat taking with them as much as they could to share with family and friends.

Fidel's plan to open rabbit restaurants throughout Cuba never materialized, though, as other more pressing priorities emerged.

Despite the kindness and generosity of most Cubans, the goal of creating a new socialist man or women would have been improbable under normal economic conditions. The Enlightenment philosopher Jean-Jacques Rousseau reflected on the enormity of that challenge:

> One who dares to undertake. . .transforming each individual, who by himself is a perfect and solitary whole, into a part of a larger whole from which he receives, in a sense, his life and his being. . .of substituting a social and moral existence for the independent and physical existence we have all received from nature. . . must, in short, take away man's own forces to give him a force that is foreign to him and that he cannot make use of without the help of others.

Can a society develop an ethos that recognizes everyone's uniqueness but also cultivates in each person a cooperative rather than an individualistic code of behavior? Both Marx and Keynes predicted that a "new man and woman" would emerge in a time of relative affluence and when the passion to accumulate capital no longer regulated how we worked and lived. And yet Fidel was attempting to create a society motivated by moral rather than material incentives when Cubans were asked to consume less to increase the capital necessary to fulfill the single-minded objective of producing ten million tons of sugar. I wondered how that decision had been made. Wouldn't a more modest plan have been less disruptive and more humane? It was not until I returned home that I discovered the answer to those questions.

The Cuban Planning Commission had been assigned the task of determining how much sugar Cuba could produce in the period between 1968 and 1969. First, they carefully reviewed how much sugar had previously been produced and carefully estimated the potential resources available to produce the sugar. Only then did the planning committee recommend the historically ambitious goal of producing eight million tons of sugar. An American economist, Edward Boorstein, who had participated in those deliberations, told me what happened next. After listening to the economists' report, Fidel had shouted, "Eight million tons is not a number we can use to mobilize the Cuban people. But ten million tons is a goal around which we can ignite their revolutionary spirit."

Astonished, I wondered how many on the planning committee grasped the social and economic burden the Cuban people would have to bear because of Fidel's audacity.

Fidel, and the advocates of revolutionary consciousness, believed that corruption within the political and economic bureaucracy was the most egregious violation of revolutionary ethics. How could such conduct be tolerated when the revolution demanded so much from Cuban people? Yet constraints on personal consumption opened opportunities for exploiting political privilege for private advantage. In 1965 and 1966 the revelation of corruption in the highest levels of government and among trade union leaders set the stage for Fidel's attack on monetary incentives and on what he called "vulgar materialism." The limited supply of consumer goods created a thriving illegal trade within the still-existing small business sector that undermined the government's dependence on moral incentives. The private sector in retail trade and the small-scale consumer industry had expanded so that it was not only supplying a growing black market but also illegally providing goods for the public sector and competing for skilled labor. To shore up Fidel's turn to moral incentives, the government decided to nationalize the remaining private enterprises in trade and industry.

I wondered whether Fidel's appeal to revolutionary *consciencia* could compete with the burden of finding the necessities people needed to meet their daily needs. Cubans began to ask whether their leaders were eating better than they were. In an environment where Cubans were forced to consume less, small differences in consumption mattered and had political consequences. Even my therapist asked me what food or drinks I was served when visiting Cuban leaders.

The Isle of Pines, soon to be called the Isle of Youth, became a showcase for many radical tourists interested in Cuba's efforts to build a communist community where the distribution of income would be based on need and not on ability. I was invited to spend a day on the Isle of Youth, where a sign proclaimed, *Why shouldn't this island be the first of communism in Cuba?*

The mission of building a communist community was assigned

to the Young Communist League, where I was told about fifty thousand youth now lived. The young communists I met were highly motivated and committed to creating a community that bore some likeness to Israeli kibbutzim. In fact, one of its economic goals was to replace Israel as the largest exporter of citrus. But as I explored the Island, I realized that the communism it sought to create depended on an ethic of work rather than an ethic of liberation. Fidel glorified the revolutionary consciousness of those young communists who "had worked a minimum of sixteen hours daily and on four occasions labored twenty-four consecutive hours." I thought this exemplified the asceticism of a monastery, not the liberation from toil that Marx foresaw in his vision of a communist future.

While I was impressed by the enthusiasm and dedication of these young radicals, their living arrangements raised some troublesome questions about the community they were creating. When I learned that most of the young people living on the Island were women, I asked how such an unequal gender distribution of labor would affect the building of a communist community.

The young woman who responded dismissed the question with a knowing grin. "Why," she asked, "do Americans always ask such questions? Women have more important things to deal with than gender equality. In Cuba woman have the same rights as men and the government provides childcare, so women can participate equally in working for the revolution." When I persisted in asking about housing and childcare arrangements on the Island, she said plans were being developed to deal with those family issues. Building a model communist community was evidently more a vision than a reality, and geographically and politically distant from what was happening on the mainland.

Upon returning to Havana, I received a dinner invitation from the anthropologist Oscar Lewis and his wife Ruth Maslow. I was told that, after reading Lewis' book on Mexican poverty, Fidel had invited them to come to Cuba to write about the Cuban revolution's efforts to eradicate poverty.

The elegant home I entered was in stark contrast to how most Cubans lived. When I arrived, I was told that Lewis was away, attending to some unexpected problems that needed his attention. The meal that was served to the economist Samuel Bowles and to our families would have been unimaginable for the most Cubans. Separate waiters served the specially prepared food and wine. The subject of poverty was never raised, but the setting and the dinner served to highlight the declining living conditions of ordinary Cubans.

Nor would Oscar Lewis be permitted to complete his research. Fidel suddenly stopped the project and confiscated most of his data in June 1970. I wondered whether the large research grant he had received from the Ford Foundation played a role in that decision. It was a time of increasing sensitivity to criticism of the revolution. Fidel terminated the project because Lewis' research disclosed that a culture of poverty still existed in Cuba.

Oscar Lewis died of a heart attack soon after leaving Cuba. I wondered whether the tensions and anxieties that he encountered while trying to complete his research had contributed to his death.

Cuba's war on poverty was in many ways successful. The poor of Cuba were the major beneficiaries of the revolution. Steady employment, and an expansive social safety net, had made their life more predictable and secure. But it was a limited victory. I could still see the shacks of the extremely poor from my apartment window and in other neighborhoods in Havana. For some Cubans the social and cultural conditions that contributed to poverty could not without difficulty be quickly eradicated. Most Cubans faced declining living standards as the government implemented its ambitious and demanding economic strategy. The variety of food products that were still available during initial years of the revolution disappeared. This was not what Che Guevara had imagined when he proclaimed: "With the poor of the earth, I will cast my lot, as Marti said, and that is what we have done. . .and here we shall remain. . . destroying all injustice and establishing a new social order."

It was becoming increasingly evident that revolutionary determination alone could not raise living standards when so much was demanded of the Cuban people. Workers were asked to work more and consume less at a time when political decisions, rather than sound economic policies, guided the organization of labor. To cope with inefficiencies, managers depended on the workers' willingness to work overtime without additional compensation. As a result, productivity declined, and absenteeism and theft increased. Is this what happens when appeals to *"consciencia"* fail to inspire the efficient use of labor? Was Cuba using coercion when moral incentives failed to inspire the effective use of the workers' labor?

My own experiences added to my concerns. I learned after working for a few hours on a hot, sunny day that cutting sugar cane is arduous and demanding work. Voluntary workers, despite their good intentions, had neither the experience nor the stamina for such work. Many of Cuba's sugar cane cutters, seeking better jobs and living conditions, had moved to other regions of the country. To fulfill the goal of producing ten million tons of sugar, Cuba was using skilled urban workers to do jobs for which they were not suited or trained.

Les Rice and his wife came to Cuba hoping to contribute their knowledge and skills to improve Cuban agriculture. I knew something of Rice's music but nothing about his farming skills. Les was the composer of the song, "The Banks Are Made of Marble," a popular ballad among the left in the United States. I spent a day with him and his wife on a farm where they produced a variety of specialty crops, mainly for export. At the time of my visit more than a hundred high school students were picking strawberries, a crop not available to ordinary Cubans. I should not have been surprised that the students seemed to be eating more than they were harvesting. Their voluntary work appeared more like a fun day in the countryside than an act of revolutionary commitment. I ate a few strawberries as well and still remember how wonderful they tasted.

Les, and especially his wife, were not pleased. They worried about the waste and how undisciplined the young students were. This was not the best way to harvest a crop. Our conversation touched on more serious problems facing Cuban agriculture. Farming, they explained, requires special knowledge about the land and the best time for planting and fertilizing and harvesting a crop. The timing of those activities was important. But those decisions were out of their control, made instead by bureaucrats in Havana who knew nothing about what was needed at any moment. Les and Ruth were committed to the revolution but were dismayed by the inefficiencies they experienced in operating their farm.

Visits to Cuban factories only confirmed widespread organizational inefficiencies and their troublesome consequences for Cuban workers. There were no financial signals to guide management decision-making, and managers had limited input in determining production targets or controlling their costs. The scarcity of spare parts and raw materials meant frequent work stoppages. As a result, managers were primarily concerned with mobilizing work effort rather than the effective and considerate use of the workers' working time.

The reliance on the workers' conscience encouraged the wasteful use of a worker's labor since managers were not under any pressure to complete tasks during normal working hours. Nor did they feel compelled to explore ways of reducing production inefficiencies. Managers frequently acted as if voluntary work was costless and could be used whenever necessary to cover disruptions in production. They seemed perplexed when I asked if they might be wasting the workers' *"consciencia"* in their efforts to fulfill their output goals.

I walked around a textile factory late one afternoon and noticed workers sitting on double decker beds. I asked the manager why they were there. He said he was waiting for a shipment of cotton that was promised but had not yet arrived. When I asked why the workers were not sent home, he replied that they were there to show their support for the revolution. Many had spent the night in the factory, ready to work when called upon.

Trade unions assisted management in their efforts to enforce work discipline and help mobilize voluntary work especially in agriculture. After attending a few trade union meetings, it became evident to me that protecting workers' rights was not the primary concern of trade unions. While they provided recreational and some social welfare benefits, trade unions did not play an important role in the lives of workers.

Problems of work discipline and absenteeism were exacerbated by factors beyond the workplace. While walking with the director of the Bank of Pinar Del Rio, I casually asked if he was concerned that workers' wages were increasing but their productivity was declining. His response surprised me. "What workers are paid does not concern us, since we control the consumption fund." I assumed he meant how much funding was available for producing and importing consumer goods. I was astonished. He seemed not to grasp the negative consequence such a policy would have on worker morale and productivity. What about the time spent waiting on line searching for scarce consumer goods, and the illegal behavior it promoted?

When wages are insufficient to purchase necessities, both moral as well as material incentives are ineffective. The Nobel Prize-winning economist Vasily Leontief warned after his visit to Cuba that inducing ordinary workers to work productively would not succeed unless there is "a steady flow of material benefits closely commensurate with the results of his individual effort." Nor, I thought, could moral incentives work in an environment where the struggle to find and buy consumer goods was degrading personal and civic life. It was in this frame of mind that I went to speak with Carlos

Raphael Rodriguez, the Minister of the Economy and Cuba's Vice President.

He greeted me warmly. His direct and candid responses to my questions disarmed me. He seemed genuinely interested in my observations about the Cuban economy. I began by conveying how impressed I was with the effort to mobilize the Cuban population to achieve Cuba's ambitious economic goals. But then I paused and conveyed my many misgivings about the social and economic costs it was imposing on workers and consumers. I spoke about the absence of economic discipline and an economy that was operating without the guidance of either the market or an effective plan.

To my surprise he nodded in seeming agreement.

Cautiously I began to speak about the limited direction and control managers seemed to have over production decisions. I wondered how moral incentives could possibly work under those economic conditions. I spoke about illusions of some who conflated the decline in the value of money with the creation of a communist society. I then told him about my recent conversation with the Director of the Bank of Pinar Del Rio. I remember pausing and saying, "Did he really believe what he was telling me?"

His response surprised me. "The tragedy is that he does believe it." I felt tears welling up in my eyes. I wondered if he saw them. Without much prompting, he began to speak about the deterioration of effective management of the Cuban economy. The absence of real economic planning, he contended, was weakening the effectiveness of moral incentives. Social consciousness was Cuba's most precious resource and must not be wasted. "Cuba," he said, "must begin to calculate the cost of social consciousness."

Encouraged by his remarks I asked when he thought Cuba would become a socialist society. He laughed and said, "Perhaps in five years, but we must act decisively if the revolution is to succeed." He then paused and added, "There is a difference between devotion to our revolution and what is required to do the frequently monotonous day-to-day work required in the economy. But to work, and to work effectively, are not one and the same thing."

To reinforce his argument, I told him about my encounter with the Centennial Youth Brigade that Fidel had championed. I said that the young communist leaders of the brigade were articulate defenders of the work of the brigade. But unlike the young communist leaders, the hundred or so teenager brigadiers I encountered seemed subdued and hesitant when I asked them why they had volunteered to join the brigade. Some simply said it was a choice between serving in the military or in the brigade. It was clear that most were there because they had no clear alternative. Fidel had proclaimed that the progress of the country depended on work of the people. But how, I asked, could these passive and somewhat frightened teenagers be expected to work productively to complete the task to which they were assigned?

I left the interview convinced that the economic problems I had seen were in no small measure due to Fidel's unrealistic radical economic goals. Efforts to rapidly deploy workers and machinery to critically needed projects, frequently outside a worker's normal working hours, undermined worker productivity as well as the workers' morale. Fidel's mobilization model depended on political leadership rather than the effective organization of work. But the effective management of work had broken down.

I would soon learn that the military under Fidel's personal command was being mobilized to help complete economic tasks, especially in the sugar harvest. Carlos Raphael Rodriguez confirmed what I was witnessing. The mass mobilization of labor was undermining work norms, the wage structure, and the value of cost accounting. As the fragile planning apparatus crumbled, the revolutionary offensive began to resemble the characteristics of a military campaign.

I learned more about the militarization of the economy from Miguel, a captain in the army and a friend of a young woman I had recently interviewed. Helena directed nursery schools that differed significantly from those organized by the Federation of Cuban Women that my younger daughter attended. Based on the curriculum of nursery schools she had observed in Sweden, her schools were less structured, providing children with more opportunities for creative and spontaneous exploration.

Miguel and Helena nodded in acknowledgement as I began recounting some of my recent visits to Cuban factories. Miguel suddenly interrupted me and said, "Bert, you have to promise me that you will not use what I am about to tell you to harm Cuba." Shaking his hand, I gave him my assurances.

He then began describing how the military and the militias were being mobilized to fulfill Cuba's economic goals. Cuba, he said, could not rely on voluntary labor to harvest ten million tons of sugar or other crops. Nor could the leadership depend on the existing planning system. The use of the military had become essential in fulfilling Cuba's economic goals. I asked whether this was an efficient solution to Cuba's economic difficulties. He shook his head. The army could not do everything that was needed. The use of the military was only a stop-gap response to Cuba's economic problems.

Miguel revealed what was most troublesome about Fidel's "revolutionary offensive." The mass mobilization of labor, and the militarization of the economy, were undermining the efficient day-to-day management of work routines, disrupting production, especially in the non-sugar sectors of the economy. How could moral incentives inspire workers when their labor was inefficiently used and wasted?

The mobilization and militarization of labor posed another fundamental problem. It provided little opportunity for workers to participate in decisions that were affecting their work and family lives. Trade unions had virtually disappeared as defenders of worker's rights and living standards. I asked whether many workers felt that their sacrifices were subverted or misused. He agreed—and was disturbed by what he was observing.

Not all my encounters with Cuban leaders were so revealing and disturbing. One memorable moment occurred during an interview with Fabio Grobart, the editor of the journal Cuba *Socialista* and a founding leader of Cuba's Communist Party. I was not sure what to expect from a meeting that Estie and Ernesto had arranged. I certainly did not anticipate Grobart beginning our conversation by asking, "*Wus denks du fun Herbert Marcuse*" (what's your opinion of Herbert Marcuse). I laughed. I never imagined that one of my first interviews with a Cuban leader would be conducted in Yiddish. I smiled and said, "A Lantzman!"

It soon became clear that Gobart was interviewing me rather

my interviewing him. I wondered whether Marcuse's book, *Soviet Communism*, which I had lent to a Cuban economist I had befriended, might be the reason for Gobart's question. But as the discussion unfolded it became clear that he was particularly interested in my opinions about the New Left. I told him that most young American radicals, while supportive of the Cuban revolution, were also highly critical of Soviet communism. When I spoke about the new left's commitment to ideals of democratic participation, Fabio interrupted and said, "Democratic participation for whom? Certainly not those who want to destroy our revolution."

Carlos, who would become a close advisor to the Chilean President Salvador Allende, posed a similar question during a conversation we had in Ernesto's apartment. "Why," he asked, "are all communist countries single-party states led by authoritarian leaders?" Ernesto responded with the standard answer that such leadership was necessary to protect the revolution from attempts by the old ruling elites to bring back the old order.

I would see Carlos again in September 1971 in Santiago, Chile, at a conference organized by the Allende government to explore the Chilean road to socialism. A central question explored at the conference was whether Chile knew how to develop a democratic path to socialism. I met Salvador Allende during the opening day of the conference. Unlike Fidel, he projected in his demeanor the formalities of his elected office. Nothing in my brief encounter with him suggested that he was a leader of a movement attempting to radically alter Chile's social and economic institutions. Allende's Socialist Party had won the presidency as part of a coalition of leftist parties that came to power with a plurality of thirty-six per cent of the vote. And yet, seated next to me at the conference, was a young exuberant Minister of Education committed to the radical reform of the Chilean economy and society.

I was asked to explore some lessons Chile might take away from Cuba's transition to socialism. At the time of the conference Chile had begun to experience economic difficulties. The price of copper, its main export, was declining. When Chile nationalized its copper industry, the United States imposed credit restrictions, forcing Chile to look to the Soviet Union for economic assistance. The United States also began providing political and economic assistance to groups opposing the Allende government. Could this be a replay of the Cuban experience?

At the conference I stressed the importance of mobilizing the participation of the Chilean people in the government's efforts to reform economy. But I asked whether divisions within the left coalition, and efforts by the United States to foment worker opposition, posed a serious challenge to Chile's democratic path to socialism.

One telling moment in the conference revealed the Allende government's commitment to a democratic transition to socialism. I listened attentively when the communist Senator Volodia Teitelboim warned of the possibility of a military coup. But the socialists in attendance dismissed his concerns, voicing confidence in Chile's democratic traditions, which they argued made a democratic path to socialism possible.

Two years later General Augusto Pinochet would overthrow the Allende government. Carlos, Ernesto's friend, died defending Allende, as did thousands of others. Allende used the rifle Fidel had given him to take his own life. The inscription on the rifle read, *To my good friend Salvador from Fidel, who by different means tries to achieve the same goals.*

Unlike my encounters with Chilean government officials, my experiences with the North Korean delegation to Cuba was in retrospect farcical. At the request of the North Korean ambassador, our families were invited to view a Korean film followed by a luncheon at the Korean embassy. It was a time of escalating tensions between the United States and North Korea. At ten in the morning, we walked into an empty movie theatre to watch a film about an idyllic and peace-loving North Korea. It was noon when the film ended. We were then driven to the embassy, where women served a luncheon of Korean delicacies while our host encouraged the men to drink the vodka that they poured into our glasses. There was endless toasting that stopped when I turned over my glass. The Koreans were clearly trying to get me drunk. I wondered what they wanted.

Two days later, I had the answer. A delegation came to my apartment with a special offer: They invited me to visit their country to report on life in North Korea. I told them I couldn't leave my family, and that I needed to complete my research. They persisted somewhat unpleasantly, insisting that going to Korea was more important than my other obligations. To end the conversation, I told them that Jose Yglesias, a reporter for the *New York Times,* was in Havana and would be better suited to undertake such an assignment. It worked. They quickly departed.

Jose appeared in our apartment a couple of days later. Somewhat agitated, he told me the following story. He had gone to sleep early the previous night but was suddenly awakened by loud banging on his door. He opened the door to two North Koreans, who insisted on speaking to him. It was impossible to refuse. What happened next, he said, was bizarre. "Without any explanation, they insisted I visit North Korea. I refused. I had difficulty getting them to leave." He laughed when I told him I was responsible for their visit.

Was the invitation to meet with Eldridge Cleaver, a prominent leader in the Black Panther Party, connected to my encounters with the North Koreans? I would learn later that Cleaver had also been contacted by the North Koreans—and had accepted their invitation to travel to their country. Marvin and I entered Cleaver's apartment in a high-rise building near the Havana Libre. He was seated in a chair, holding a pistol, shifting it from one hand to the other. Standing behind him was another Black man who we were told had recently hijacked an American airplane. The two men eyed us suspiciously as we sat down to talk.

Cleaver had been a recent candidate for president on the Peace and Freedom Party ticket but was at that moment a fugitive charged with assaulting three Oakland police officers. Since he had found a haven in Cuba, I assumed he would be a strong supporter of the Cuban revolution. Surprisingly, the opposite was closer to the truth. When asked about his impressions of Cuba, he responded defiantly. "Cuba is still a racist society. Cuba claims that they have eliminated racism, but that's a lie. Blacks are treated better here, but racism is still a big problem. It's not a coincidence that so much attention is paid to Jose Marti, the white hero of Cuban independence, while the role of the Black leader Antonio Maceo is neglected.

Why are there only seven or eight Blacks among the top leaders of the revolution?"

His anger was palpable. "Despite what you are told, Blacks make up most of the Cuban population, but the composition of the government is mainly White. And when you ask why, you get the old argument that there aren't enough educated Black people." He then paused and went on, "If I had a match, I would burn down the Havana Libre." His resentment puzzled me. After all, Cuba had provided protection against incarceration by American authorities. When I left the apartment, I turned to Marvin and said, "Cleaver seems unhinged. Why was he holding a gun in his hand?"

"No," he replied, "you just need to look into his eyes to see his honesty."

Was there an explanation for Cleaver's strange behavior? After I left Cuba, I learned about some possible reasons for his anger. He felt the Cuban's had broken promises they made to help the Black Panthers establish a radio station in Havana to broadcast their revolutionary ideas. Was Cleaver just another example of disappointed expectation, something quite familiar to me? Whatever the sources of his discontent, his behavior contributed to some of the absurdities of life in Cuba.

I often wonder whether watching the film *Marat/Sade* one sunny afternoon at the end June sparked my decision to leave Cuba earlier than I had originally planned. I knew nothing about the film Peter Brook had made from a Peter Weiss play. I was one of a select group of artists and intellectuals who had been invited to a private screening of the film. Watching the movie, I wondered whether it would ever be seen by ordinary Cubans. Weiss's imagined account of the assassination of Jean-Paul Marat, by inmates of an insane asylum, vividly recorded the crazed inmates' call for revolution and captured my imagination, as did the confrontation between the revolutionary Marat and the cynical libertarian the Marquis de Sade. I fixated on those inmates watching Marat and Sade thrash out their ideas to stinging affect while the inmates reacted with crazed shrieks against injustice, demanding, "We want our revolution *now!*"

Blinded momentarily by the sun as I left the theatre, I looked to see whether others felt the same sting of the film. I wondered whether they too thought they were living in a surreal world. I realized as I walked home that it was time to leave Cuba. I needed to be in an environment where I could more clearly and independently evaluate the changing face of the Cuban revolution. Eduardo smiled when I told him about my decision to leave. "Bert," he said, "the anxiety you experienced in Cuba will disappear when you return to New York."

It would take almost three weeks before arrangements could be made for my family and me to travel home on a Soviet freighter bound for Montreal. We gave the Bravos the Volkswagen we had shipped to Cuba. I loaded two large trunks with research materials, not knowing how I would get them into the United States. I boarded the freighter with mixed feelings: sad that I had not fully accomplished what I had set out do, but comforted that, when I returned home, I would be able to reevaluate the hopes I had about Cuba's revolution.

The Soviet freighter delayed its departure for a week because a shipment of sugar scheduled for delivery to Canada had not arrived. The ship ultimately left without the sugar, a parting example of the mounting inefficiencies of the Cuban economy. The absence of the sugar made the freighter more vulnerable to the movement of the ocean, blemishing what was otherwise a relaxing ocean voyage.

I did try unsuccessfully to interact with the crew by playing some Soviet songs on my mandolin. But crew members had evidently been told not to engage with us. We were the only passengers. We ate our three meals in a special dining area reserved for the captain and the first mate, who lived separately and more comfortably than those they managed. I could see the Florida shores from the deck of the Soviet freighter as it rocked from side to side in the choppy Atlantic Ocean.

It was otherwise a pleasant four-day journey. Seated at the captain's table, we were served food I had not eaten since leaving New York. The dark bread, herring, butter, cheese, and soups reminded me of the food of my childhood. As the freighter moved down the St. Lawrence River toward Montreal, I wondered where I might store my many boxes of research documents. Fortunately, a Canadian security officer who boarded the ship and checked our passports and belongings knew of a warehouse nearby where I could safely leave my research materials. When this was done, we took a taxi to the airport, where to my surprise two friends from New York greeted us. Marcel looked at me and asked, "Are you okay? You've lost so much weight."

Chapter 6

THE ETHICS OF CONVICTION
AND THE ETHICS OF RESPONSIBILITY

ACCORDING TO THE HISTORIAN E.H. CARR, the moral principles that guide our behavior are like checks with printed and blank parts. On the printed part we find words like justice, equality, liberty, and democracy, but the check has no value until we fill in how much of these ideals we wish to spend. Only then do we know how much justice, equality, liberty, and democracy we want to allocate and to whom they should be given.

I was pushed to rewrite one of those checks after receiving an unexpected call from an old friend. I had recently returned from Cuba and had not been in touch with Herb for several years. I was therefore surprised when he called to say he was flying in from Seattle and needed to speak to me. In a somber and somewhat tense voice, he told me there was something very important he wanted to share with me.

Herb had a dramatic side to his persona, so I was not concerned by his unexpected and somewhat puzzling request to meet. I liked Herb. He was warm and engaging but at times could be overly dramatic when talking about politics or everyday experiences. We agreed to meet in a restaurant in Greenwich Village not far from an apartment he and his partner Merrill had rented when he lived in New York.

It seemed as if nothing had changed as he approached my table smiling broadly. He asked how I was doing, and without much prompting I began describing my Cuban experiences and the personal and political challenges I had encountered. He listened and asked some questions. But I sensed he had something more important he needed to discuss. I looked at him and said, "Enough about me. What's going on with you?"

He stared at me somberly and said, "I came to tell you that I am not the person you think I am." He paused and then exclaimed, "I'm gay, and I want to tell you why I hid this essential part of who I am from all those who have meant so much to me."

I don't recall my exact response. I wasn't surprised. I had had some suspicions but dismissed them because he'd been living with a woman when he was in New York. I told him how sorry I was that he had waited so long to tell me. His story touched me deeply because, while living in Cuba, I too experienced feelings of isolation and exclusion. As he began describing his troubling journey, I realized that Herb was on his own search for belonging and recognition. Shuleh and Camp Kinderland had connected him to his Jewish roots, but he had continued to feel misunderstood. He exclaimed with pride how the New Left, the Civil Rights Movement, and an emerging Women's Movement, but especially the Gay Rights Movement, had helped him find the support he needed to live openly as a gay man.

Herb assured me of his commitment to what he believed were our shared values. But he needed to align his principles more closely with his identity as a gay man. Passionately he declared, "I'm not a worker, so I can't join the Labor Movement. I'm not a woman, so I can't be part of the Women's Movement, and I'm not Black, so I can't be part of the Black Power Movement. But I am a gay man, and it is only as a gay man that I can express my deepest political convictions."

I responded sympathetically, but I wondered what the political consequences would be if every group sought its own way of cashing E.H. Carr's checks. Did we need a broader set of principles that would unite all individuals seeking social justice and recognition?

It did not take too long after returning from Cuba to realize that the times were really changing. In 1967, a year before I left for Cuba, thousands of people had marched on the Pentagon, and while I was in Cuba nearly three hundred thousand had protested near the White House. Nixon's decision to escalate the Vietnam War at the end of April 1970 pulled me into what became the largest student protest in American history. At the beginning of May, four million young people joined rallies that shut down hundreds of colleges and high schools throughout the country. The strikes revealed to a new politically engaged generation the power of collective action.

Nixon's escalation of the war, with its massive bombings and deployment of troops into Cambodia, ignited strikes among students everywhere. The subsequent killing of four Kent State University students brought the protest movement to Hofstra University, where I was teaching. My year in Cuba had tested my own beliefs and values. The sociologist Max Weber distinguished between an "ethics of moral conviction" and an "ethics of responsibility." Fidel had turned to revolutionary consciousness to mobilize the Cuban people. I had witnessed the significant social cost of Fidel's revolutionary ethics. Standing before the almost 2000 Hofstra students who had walked out of their classes to protest America's involvement in the Vietnam war, I felt the mobilizing power of the ethics of conviction. As I listened to speakers denounce the expansion of the Vietnam War and the killing of innocent students, I wondered what could be done.

Some students and faculty saw the university as contributing to a powerful corporate military state that was undermining our democratic institutions. They called on students to strike and stop attending classes. They established a communication network in the Student Center to organize strike activities. Some students resisted, organizing under the banner of Strike Back. They demanded that the university keep classes in session. In the face of the growing turmoil, including a student sit-in at the University Faculty Club, Clifford Lord, the university president, briefly suspended classes. Students mulled in the courtyard, debating how they should respond.

Stepping up to the podium, I had to quickly decide whether to support the strike or to find another way of engaging the university. I don't remember my exact words, but I decided that ending classes, while a more radical choice, was not the best course of action. I began speaking about of my year in Cuba, describing the revolution's attempts to mobilize the Cuban people to their radical economic goals. But I noted that, when not efficiently planned, the Cuban workers' commitment to the revolution was weakened. I warned that, unless we organized effectively, we would not be able to sustain the momentum of our protest. I did not want the demonstration to end without a plan of action. I called on students and faculty to meet in a building off the quad to discuss what needed to be done. It was the first step in the creation of an alternative university.

For many of us who assembled that afternoon, the path forward seemed clear. We believed that, unless classes resumed, most students would leave the campus, ending their engagement in the protest. Our plan was more ambitious. We decided to create an alternative university during the final month of classes. A faculty–student committee was created to develop new courses and engage the Hofstra community in political and cultural events. During these activities, I was invited by President Lord to meet with his staff. It was a moment of turmoil and uncertainty. It was clear that the administration was under considerable pressure to ensure students and their families that classes would restart, and that planned graduation ceremonies would take place. Given these circumstances I believed we had considerable leverage in shaping the conditions for resuming classes.

The meeting began affably, but the ambiance quickly changed

when it became evident that the administration's primary objective was to end student protest. They spoke about our responsibilities to students and their families, and the need for a return to normalcy. I told them to listen more carefully to the concerns of students and faculty and warned that they could not act as if nothing had happened. I then presented our proposal for ending the strike. We would support the resumption of classes but only under certain conditions. Students would be permitted to enroll in alternative courses that departments developed to complete the Spring semester. We also insisted that students be allowed to participate in assemblies and protests during this period.

I was surprised how quickly the administration agreed to our demands. But they insisted that students' grades be based on work completed through the first week in May. The final agreement gave faculty considerable flexibility in evaluating students. Grading had become particularly difficult because averting military service depended on maintaining an acceptable academic standing. Grade inflation was an inevitable consequence. After all, those were extraordinary times.

A list of some courses that faculty developed suggests the tenor of the moment: "Imperialism," "The Death of Democracy," "Non-Violence in Political Change," "The Possibility of Revolution in America." Other courses offered a broader look at society and culture: "Science, Technology and Humanity," "The American Political System: Responsive or Not," "Black Consciousness." We organized music, theater, and art performances, and our Political Action Committee engaged students in workshops, encouraging them to participate in political activity.

Were we radical enough? Evidently not for those faculty and students who thought ending classes and joining the striking students from other colleges on Long Island and around the country was the only political action to take. I remember meeting with Clifford Lord in the student dining room when Jerry Rosenfeld, an anthropology professor and an old friend from the Bronx, approached, shouting, "I thought you were a radical!" I wondered what he thought radicalism meant. Did he consider the defiant gesture of Norman Coleman, a then-Hofstra student, radical? Coleman had destroyed his radio and phonograph at a strike rally. While I thought our consumerist culture was undermining our social responsibilities as citizens, I thought Coleman's act naïve. I mention this because Coleman would later serve one term as the Republican Senator from Minnesota.

Those heady times inspired visions of new possibilities. John Lennon's song "Imagine" captured that moment of renewed utopian hopes, insisting that he wasn't the only person with dreams. But my utopian dreams were changing. My vision of the future had become more grounded in the possible—no more "pie in the sky by and by" but an attainable future that would change the way we worked and lived; a radical vision that carefully considered the social cost of change. Ignoring the connection between the rate of change and the cost of change, I now believed, caused avoidable harm to those whose lives one wanted to improve, something I had learned from my experiences in Cuba.

And yet my quiescent dreams of a better world had been reignited. Feelings of isolation that I'd experienced in Cuba had faded. The renewal of radical politics revived new debates about the role of workers as agents of social and political change. Labor historians began to revise our understanding of the diverse social and cultural history of the working class. I wondered whether a new phase of capitalist development was unfolding. The rediscovery of inequality and alienation stimulated a revival of research on the working class. Was the old working class being absorbed into an expanding middle class? Had an emerging post-industrial society produced a "new" working class? What was the connection of race and gender to changes in class structures? How was the educational system adapting to changing demands of work in an evolving post-industrial capitalist society?

My friend and colleague Murray Yanowitch and I explored these questions in our book *The Worker in Post-Industrial Capitalism: Radical and Liberal Responses*. In 1974, a few months after our book was published, I organized a meeting in the office of the *Monthly Review,* a Marxist magazine edited by Paul Sweezy, to discuss Harry Braverman's recently published book *Labor and Monopoly Capitalism*. I had met Harry in Cuba and thought his book raised important questions about the nature of work and the role of workers as agents of change. I was therefore taken aback when the political scientist Frances Fox Piven opened the discussion by asking Harry, "Why do you assume that work is central in the lives of workers?"

Astonished, he snapped, "Well, if you don't believe that, there is no point in discussing my book." Frances' question reflected the knowledge she had gained from defending poor women on welfare who often preferred to stay home to care for their children rather than participate in the workforce.

I thought Frances was raising a more general question about the changing meaning of work in affluent capitalist societies. If work had become so degraded, why would workers view it as intrinsic rather than a means of reaping the rewards of an expanding consumer culture? Had the corporation found an effective way of diffusing worker militancy? In an article about the British working-class, Eric Hobsbawm warned that "the forward march of labor had halted." And in a soon-to-be- published book, the French intellectual Andre Gorz would proclaim that we should "say good-bye to the working-class."

A meeting with the provost of Hofstra University in 1973 pulled me more directly into the debates about workers and the changing nature of work. The provost was seeking ways of expanding the visibility of the university at a moment when student enrollment was falling. He asked if I was interested in creating a cultural center that would reach out to the larger Long Island community. My response surprised him. "The problems that workers face today is of greater concern to me. I would be interested in developing a *labor* center that examines the changing nature of work in post-industrial society."

He looked at me and calmly said, "Do it. You have my support."

Shortly after the meeting, the Center for Labor and Democracy was launched. An unexpected call from Leo Kaplan would determine its initial activities. Leo asked if Hofstra University might be interested in developing a college program for workers in Manhattan. David Livingston, the President of District 65, a division of the Distributive Workers of America, had approached him about creating a college program for his members, but the Cooper Union faculty had rejected the idea. "Why don't you call David Livingston to see what he has in mind?" The idea seemed implausible but intriguing.

The *hecher curson* held its classes in the union headquarters, and that was where I heard Pete Seeger, Harry Belafonte, and other folk singers perform. When I was on the faculty of the Cooper Union, I often went to 13 Astor Place for lunch. Entering District 65's headquarters rekindled those youthful memories. I asked my colleague and collaborator Murray Yanowitch to join me to help avoid any misunderstanding about what could be done. We took the elevator to the seventh floor and entered a large open space where union leaders had their desks. Unlike the business agents in the ILGWU, those who worked directly with the membership were called organizers. We walked past a bustle of activity to the end of the large hall to David Livingston's office.

The ambiance changed dramatically when we entered that spacious wood-paneled office. David Livingston, seated behind a large desk, welcomed us. I noticed a large picture of a turtle on the wall with a caption that read, *The turtle can't move forward without sticking out its neck.* I smiled but was tempted to say that it was a also time when the turtle was most vulnerable.

I must have touched the right note when I began our conversation with stories about my links to the union stretching back to my childhood. His demeanor changed from somewhat cautious to more inviting. I told him about my conversation with Leo Kaplan and why the idea of creating a college program for workers intrigued me. But I thought the distance separating our institutions made such an affiliation unworkable. Anticipating my skepticism, he exclaimed, "Bring your campus to our headquarters."

Somewhat taken aback, I responded, "Well, that opens up possibilities we haven't considered."

What he said next would change the course of my academic life. "We are prepared," he said, "to devote an entire floor of our headquarters to create the classrooms and offices you need to set up a college for our members, and we will pay for its construction." He spoke about the union's democratic tradition, reminding me that the headquarters was a place where members came for dental care and other social services, and where retirees assembled to share experiences. David spoke of a time when union members came to the headquarters to participate in cultural and political activities. They rejected checking off wages to pay union dues because they wanted to bring the membership into the building. With a smile, he asked, "Why can't Hofstra University come to our headquarters?"

"Okay," I said, "let's see if this can be done." Walking out of the union headquarters that day, I was uncertain what the university's response would be.

But I could not have moved forward without the participation of Alice Kessler-Harris. I met Alice while chairing a meeting of Hofstra University's anti-war committee. She approached me asking, "What can I do to help?" Her enthusiasm was disarming.

"Who are you?" I asked. She told me she taught in the history department, but it would take the next few weeks for a more complete answer to unfold.

One exchange was particularly surprising. "So, what have you been working on?"

She casually said, "Jewish Immigration to the United States at the end of the 19th century."

I responded, "But you would need to know Yiddish."

"Yes," she said.

"You're Jewish?" I asked.

After Alice agreed to work with me, whatever doubts I had about its feasibility faded. But constructing a college campus in a trade union headquarters, and developing a new degree program, were more difficult than I initially imagined. It would require obtaining the support of the Hofstra University faculty and administration as well as the approval of the New York State Department of Education. It would also depend on the ability of the union to obtain paid release time from work for workers attending the program.

What I did not anticipate was the resistance I would encounter from Hofstra's faculty.

Standing on a stage at a meeting of the faculty, I was startled when a professor of history asked, "Why does Hofstra need to create a new degree program in a union headquarters in Manhattan? It seems fishy and inconsistent with the goals of a liberal arts degree."

Others among the faculty seemed to agree. I had begun thinking of a response when, unexpectedly, a respected member of the faculty spoke up. "Of course, it's a fishy program. That's why it offers a Bachelors in Applied Social Science, or BASS." Laughter erupted, diffusing the tension in the room, and despite some hesitancy the program was approved.

Unlike more traditional labor studies programs, we envisioned a college that enhanced the critical skills workers needed to become more effective participants and leaders in their union, workplace, and community. While offering a variety of career paths, we encouraged our students to use their education to further a more just society. Those objectives were met by some with skepticism and at times with disapproval and enmity.

Were our goals utopian? Clearly our approach to worker education conflicted with the dominant meritocratic ideology. We recognized that most of the students who enrolled in our college program did so because they wanted to find better-paying jobs that offered greater economic security and recognition. But as our advisory committee noted we hoped that their "competence as citizens, as educated men and women, as participants in the life of their union will be the principal channels through which their educational experience will find expression." Building on the practical knowledge of our students. we hoped to engage our worker-students in an innovative learning environment. It was a vision that guided and sustained us against considerable odds.

In an article on August 29, 1974, the *New York Times* announced, "Workers Are Set to Go to Hofstra. The new program, a collaborative venture by Hofstra University and District 65, is designed to provide working people with new opportunities to obtain competence and expertise for leadership roles in labor unions, the community and society at large."

We had overcome many obstacles. An agreement between Hofstra University's President Robert Payton, the Distributive Workers' President David Livingston, and New York State certification of the

Hofstra branch campus made it possible to begin classes in September 1976. Yet I still felt uneasy, especially after some troublesome encounters with David Livingston.

On one occasion I entered his office with great anticipation. I had just learned that we had been awarded a large government grant that I thought would cement the university's commitment to the program. I thought David had asked to see me to acknowledge the importance of a grant that legitimized our efforts and boosted the cooperation we needed from the university and employers.

I was sorely mistaken. He did not look at me as I walked into his office. Only after a long silence, while he waved a copy of the grant proposal, did I see the rage in his face. "How *dare* you write about our union. You know nothing about our union and our membership. It will take you years to get that knowledge. You have distorted who we are and what we do."

Shocked, I did not know how to respond. I reached for my briefcase, preparing to leave. Looking at him, I responded, "The government agency that gave us the grant is particularly interested in assisting poor and low-wage workers. District 65 has a long history of organizing such workers. Why should that undermine the reputation of the union?" I tried to control my anger, knowing that it would only undermine what power or dignity I still had left.

But his demeanor suddenly changed. It was as if he had turned off a switch. He simply nodded and began inquiring about the benefits the union would receive from the grant. His impulsive behavior should have forewarned me about what happened next.

The program was scheduled to begin in September 1976. The tenth floor of the Union Headquarters had been transformed into a new learning center. When I discovered that David owned a summer cottage not too far from a house I had recently purchased in the Berkshires, I organized a meeting of Hofstra faculty and union leaders in the Berkshires to help cement the cooperation we needed to move forward.

After a pleasant dinner at a local inn, we assembled in my house. The atmosphere was festive. I asked my daughter Julie to lead us in singing union songs. At that moment I felt we were creating something important, perhaps an innovative way of providing a college education for workers.

David abruptly ended those lofty thoughts. Without any warning he abruptly announced, "I don't think we can begin the program in September."

Everyone was taken aback. David seemed to enjoy our confusion and discomfort. Was this his way of telling us that nothing could be done without his approval?

I repressed my anger and said, "The university has planned for a September opening. Faculty and staff schedules have been assigned. Workers cannot so easily change the arrangements they have made to attend classes. The *New York Times* announced the start of the program. To postpone the start of the program at this late date would undermine the enthusiasm of those who have worked so hard to make this possible."

Others in the room nodded in agreement.

David grinned as if he had gotten the response he expected. "Okay," he said, "but there's much work that still needs to be done."

It was a troubling way to end the meeting. I walked Alice to her car. "I nearly lost it," I said. "Do you think this can work?"

"Who knows?" she responded. "But it's worth doing. We've started something with so many possibilities."

At that moment I realized how important Alice's support meant to me. "Yes," I said. "But I can't do this without you."

The following September something special happened on the tenth floor of the union headquarters. There was a buzz of activity and excitement as faculty and staff welcomed students to their newly constructed campus.

But some union staff were apprehensive. Some asked whether we were training their replacements. A few union staff members joined the class of 1976. It soon become clear that our newly created educational community would play an important role in the life of the union.

Many of the workers who entered the program in September were highly motivated; many were exceptional students. They brought to the program a variety of experiences in community and labor activities. Some did have deficiencies in basic skills required for college level work. We paid particular attention to those special needs, asking all faculty to participate in improving the student's writing skills. We hired counsellors to provide additional support for students who needed help in language and mathematics proficiency. While some needed special assistance to overcome past deficiencies, many were mature adults with extensive organizational experiences.

More challenging was building a learning environment where differences in race and gender could be used to unite rather than divide student loyalty. Sixty percent of our students were either

American or non-American Black. Thirteen percent were Hispanic, and twenty-seven percent were white. About sixty percent were male and forty percent female. Thirty-eight percent were over the age of thirty.

So creating a common culture of learners was not easy. It required building a community of shared values enriched by the experiences of students from different ethnic and racial backgrounds.

Some resisted, arguing that their Black identity was the lens through which they best understood their life experiences. They looked to recently liberated African countries for inspiration. While we understood the central role that race played in the lives of our Black students, we still tried to find ways of using race to unite rather than divide our community. I remember a moment when an articulate Black student challenged our efforts to create an integrated community. In response, we asked Calistus Ndlovu to speak to our students about the role of race and class in Africa. A Hofstra University history professor, Cal would shortly become Zimbabwe's Minister of Construction. In his soft-spoken voice, he explained why newly liberated African countries continued to experience the injuries of class and the importance of building broad-based coalitions to overcome racism. His intervention helped, but uniting our diverse community would be an ongoing challenge.

Our goals differed from more traditional university labor studies programs. Moving beyond the customary trade union administration and collective bargaining courses, we offered classes in the administration and delivery of human services, an area of study important for workers interested in serving their communities. We believed that, if business schools could train the leaders that corporations needed to maximize their profits, then universities should be able to help workers develop skills they needed to achieve a more democratic distribution of authority. Lofty goals indeed! We would soon discover obstacles, not only from the university, but also from the union.

I did not see it coming. A year after our founding, the dean of the college, Robert Vogt, handed me a report written by his associate dean, Robert Davison. The opening sentence began with these ominous words. "Instead of recommending the closing out of Hofstra's ties to the two institutions, I urge instead that Bert Silverman, together with Alice Harris, be removed from the administration of these projects. . .Hofstra should not continue as before. . .because the project as directed. . .has the potential of becoming a public scandal damaging our academic integrity. . .I regard Bert as the true leader and originator, and Alice as the similarly disposed subordinate." Stunned, I continued reading. "I regard as educationally subversive. . . pressure groups which attempt to impose a particular orthodoxy on the teacher such as 'this is the way it will be taught at this Yeshiva.'" Davison claimed that our goal of developing the skills workers needed to become more effective participants in their unions and workplaces undermined what he believed were the hallmarks of a liberal arts education. He was especially offended by a paper on rethinking labor studies that Alice Harris, Murray Yanowitch, and I had written. In that paper we'd argued that a democratic society was incompatible with how work was currently organized.

But the curriculum we developed was rooted in current realities and not in some yet-unrealized vision. Was developing the skills for greater democratic participation incompatible with the goals of a liberal college education? Despite Davison's claims, we were confident that the unions involved in the program supported those values and goals. Yet Davison concluded, "Indoctrination, not education, clearly is the institute's reason for being as managed by Bert and Alice." Davison believed that something sinister was happening. He suggested that I had formed a symbiotic alliance with David Livingston, that I had become a useful pawn in David's efforts to sustain the power of "his cadre of economically privileged, older cultured Jewish leaders" in a union whose membership was no longer Jewish.

I shook my head in disbelief. Davison did not know that the union leadership had been deeply engaged in the Civil Rights Movement. David and his leadership had established a close relation with Martin Luther King and played an important role in organizing the March on Washington. I wondered whether anti-Semitism had played a role in Davison's attack on us. I turned to Dean Vogt, shouting, "How could you send a report stuffed with lies and innuendos to President Shuart?"

His response did not allay my anger. "I had no choice, but don't worry—my report to the provost offers a more positive analysis of your efforts." In his comments, Vogt noted that those of us who helped create the new degree program for workers had "demonstrated an admirable degree of imagination, dedication and hard work, and they deserve our encouragement and support." Despite inevitable problems he continued, "I believe. . .the programs will make a solid contribution to higher education and to the professional credit of the people who have worked so hard to create and develop it." Still, it would soon become clear that President Shuart had become more critical and distrustful of what we were doing in Hofstra's newly created branch campus.

Our relationship with District 65's leadership, while more supportive, would soon reveal the parameters of their commitment. The success of the labor college depended on several key conditions that the union agreed to meet. The first was obtaining paid released time so that workers could become full-time students. This made it possible for students to attend afternoon classes and to receive government aid to pay the reduced Hofstra University tuition. It soon became evident, though, that the union could not afford to provide the released time from work for all students. This became more problematic when the college program expanded to include workers from District 37, the union representing New York City public service workers.

The second most important condition that District 65 said it could meet was to make available a pool of workers who met the prerequisites necessary to enroll in a college degree program. I thought David would certainly agree to opening the program to other unions. The union's New York City membership was approximately seven thousand. We could not draw the students we needed from such a small group of workers. We needed to open the college program to a larger group of workers. Why couldn't workers from District 37 attend classes at the 13 Astor Place campus? David refused.

At the meeting at which I updated David about the District 37 program and suggested we open the program to workers from other unions, his facial expression gradually changed. "Why," he shouted, "should I open the program to other unions when it is our members' dues that pay for this program?"

I responded defensively that we could charge a fee that non-65 union members would pay to participate in our program.

"No!" he said. "It would no longer be a special educational program paid for and open only to our members."

"But David," I responded, "opening the program to other unions would contribute to your efforts to organize white collar workers." I knew that the union had successfully organized clerical workers at Columbia University and some leading publishing companies. "No," he insisted. "This program will be open only to our members."

We began exploring other ways of expanding the outreach of our program. We recruited Leonard Dryansky, a professor of Dramatic Arts at the University of Syracuse, to explore the possibility of creating a workers' cabaret offering workers opportunities to see theatre and hear music on Friday and Saturday nights. Our goal was to revive a lost District 65 tradition. It would be called "Bread and Roses," named after a popular union song. Once again, I reviewed our plans with David Livingston. He listened and nodded. I thought he might support the idea. He began asking some legitimate questions. "Where would the money come from to support the program? Who would be in charge of running such an ambitious undertaking?" He didn't give us a chance to respond before he concluded, "It's beyond what we can do. Besides, it presents too many security risks for the union." I left the meeting discouraged, wondering why a progressive union was unwilling to develop a program that would expand its reach and influence.

A few months later Moe Foner, the educational director of the hospital workers' union, launched a major cultural initiative called "Bread and Roses." It received extensive coverage in the *New York Times* and other local newspapers. Frank Brown, one of the older 65 leaders, approached me with a copy of the *Times* in his hand. "Why," he asked, "didn't we do this?"

I shook my head and said, "Ask David." I would soon learn that a worker enrolled in Lenny Dryansky's class had discussed our project with Moe Foner, who, unlike David, moved quickly to create a version of our project.

Livington's resistance to our initiative to expand the cultural reach of the college program undermined our vision of what a cooperative college and trade union might achieve. It became increasingly apparent that District 65 was ill-equipped to support our broader educational goals. It soon would lose its status as an independent trade union. In 1981, District 65 affiliated with the United Automobile Worker's Union. Six years later, it was integrated into the UAW as a full-fledged department. In 1993, District 65 declared bankruptcy, its members absorbed into the UAW.

As the 1970s ended, I began to feel as if I was pushing against the grain. Trade union membership continued to decline in the face of increasing business resistance. Public support for trade unions in a time of economic uncertainty had declined. During the period of rising inflation and unemployment, trade union demands for higher wages and benefits were singled out as the major cause of our economic ills. Hope for a revived and politically engaged labor movement faded. It was also a time when my marriage began to unravel.

What had already been evident in Cuba became clearer as I grappled with conflicting feelings about ending a childhood relationship. I was caught in a dilemma that seemed impossible to untangle. While I believed that I was justified in seeking understanding and happiness in a marriage, I had been taught that a commitment to family trumped my individual pursuit of happiness. Those values began to weaken as the social and political culture radically changed and an emerging women's movement challenged traditional views about marriage and sexuality.

Traveling from Hofstra University to District 65 with Alice, I suggested that we drive to the Lower East Side to buy a knish. "What's a knish?" she asked.

I laughed. "Are you sure you're Jewish?"

Alice had become more than a partner in our efforts to create a college for workers. She was also coping with a difficult moment in her family life but was fortunate to have support from an evolving women's movement that helped her end an unhappy marriage. She spoke freely and openly about her personal life and that difficult relationship. I felt I had found someone with whom I could share my most intimate feelings and desires.

When Alice left to teach history at Warwick University in England, the sense of isolation I had experienced in Cuba began to haunt me once again. I began thinking seriously about ending my marriage. I saw more clearly that the absence of intimacy in it contributed to feelings of loneliness. But how could I end a marriage of twenty-nine years without inflicting pain on my family? I told Evie I needed a separation and agreed that we see a marriage counselor.

After a few sessions Evelyn insisted that the children also participate. It soon became clear why she wanted them there. Seated in a circle, the therapist listened as Evelyn opened the session demanding that I tell the children that it was I who wanted to end our marriage. I looked at Devi and Julie and said, "Yes, but I'm not sure it's the right thing to do."

The therapist looked at me and asked, "Why not?"

I looked at her and said, "I don't think you appreciate that I come from a culture where marriage is seen as a commitment you don't easily end."

Her response startled me. "I don't believe you. I know that culture. I think you're bluffing. You don't really want to end your marriage."

Stunned, I looked at Evie and the children for what seemed like a moment suspended in time and finally said, "I want to end my marriage."

The apartment I rented in Park Slope, Brooklyn, was large enough to accommodate my children. Everything seemed so strange and different the first night Devi and Julie were with me. I tried to assure them I would never abandon them. I asked them to hold my hand and said, "I love you and will always be there for you. We will always be together as a family." But I knew nothing I could say or do would take away the pain that I had caused them. Devi was only 13, still living at home, and had to bear the brunt of Evelyn's anger and depression. Julie, already 18, took on what should have been her mother's responsibilities. I wondered whether I had underestimated the psychological costs of my decision.

My dreams of a better world were also changing. The promises of social democracy had begun to ebb. In the late winter of 1980, *Challenge* magazine asked me to investigate the problems European welfare states were encountering. I began setting up interviews with prominent social democratic leaders and intellectuals who had played important roles in developing a middle way between capitalism and socialism. The project also provided an opportunity to see Alice and renew a relationship that I hoped might lead to a lifelong partnership.

Sweden was the first stop. For many reformers, it was the prototype of a successful social democracy. It had abandoned the revolutionary goal of socializing production, adopting instead a strategy of democratizing capitalism. After the Second World War, as living standards rose, most social democrats began to believe that a reformed market system could achieve both the goals of rising income and high employment as well as a balanced foreign trade on which Sweden depended. These golden years ended the nation's brief experiments with nationalization and planning, which had emerged in response to wartime emergencies. But when economic problems began to threaten Sweden's standard of living, what became known as the "Swedish Model" was born.

Sweden constructed a welfare state that provided generous social and financial support for a typical working-class family from the birth of their children to the care of the elderly. Children entered life with their health care, education, and retirement generously provided for. The Swedish people willingly devoted more than fifty percent of its Gross National Product to cover those costs. Moreover, when their children entered the workforce, they would almost certainly join a union, as did most workers. The wage settlements that their unions accepted were designed to reduce wage differentials to promote greater worker solidarity.

On a cool March Day, I walked down the cobbled streets of downtown Stockholm and entered the building where Gunnar Myrdal and his wife Alva lived. Myrdal was one of the founders of the Swedish welfare state. His book *An American Dilemma* had introduced him to an American audience by exposing the role that racism played in American life. His wife Alva was a feminist scholar and an important diplomat and leader in the disarmament movement. She opened the door. Smiling warmly, she ushered me to a small sitting room, where he rose to greet me. While he and I exchanged some pleasantries, she returned with coffee and some sweets.

What happened next surprised me. While I knew Myrdal was troubled by the rising influence of neo-liberalism, I had not anticipated how alarmed he was by the challenges it posed for social democracy. "It's not only the atomic bomb that is threatening the world with disaster," he exclaimed. "It's also the ideas of Milton Friedman that are now being adopted in England and the United States, and a bit in many other countries. But they will not come to Sweden."

I also had a personal stake in these interviews. I was troubled by the fading support for New Deal liberalism in the United States. I thought a review of the Swedish model might provide a deeper understanding of the problems welfare states faced. Sweden had made great strides in improving its standard of living while also creating a more egalitarian society. But cracks had opened in the foundation on which its social democratic model was built. I wondered how serious those problems were and how they were being addressed. The country's mixed economy left the management of production decisions in the hands of the owners of private enterprises. Capitalism was to be reformed, not at the point of the production, but by more equally distributing income. I soon learned that Sweden's efforts to democratize capitalism depended on a steadily growing economy.

I asked Myrdal whether he still believed that the Swedish welfare state was "more than an achieved situation. . .it had become an immutable trend."

He shook his head and said, "How could anyone predict the future in a world threatened by nuclear war?" The threat of nuclear disaster was a theme I often encountered in discussions with European intellectuals that reenforced their gloom about the rise of neo-liberal ideas and policies. I nodded in agreement, shifting the conversation by asking whether he thought the Swedish model was in crisis. Yes, he responded but not because of Sweden's social welfare policies. Inflation, he contended, was the main source of Sweden's social and economic problems. It generates a speculative psychology affecting all groups that cannot be detected by economist's mathematical models. Myrdal warned that when speculation is seen as more profitable than honest work or investment, it can destroy the social fabric of society.

I wondered whether inflation was a product of Sweden's highly organized labor market and its full-employment policies. Did this suggest a fundamental flaw in its social democratic strategy? He shook his head, insisting that it was the economic environment that had changed. The rapid economic growth that Western democra-

cies had experienced in the 1950s and the 1960s had ended. Without steady economic growth, cooperation among workers, and between trade unions and corporations, was fraying.

I learned that the foundation that supported the Swedish social
democratic model rested on three pillars. First—as I have already
mentioned—unlike the Soviet Union, Sweden's mixed economy left
production decisions largely in the hands of the managers of capital.
Capitalism was reformed, not at the point of production, but
through a more equal distribution of its increasing output of consumer goods and services. To sustain that goal, Sweden's distributional socialism depended on a second pillar: the steady growth of
the economic pie that allowed the simultaneous expansion of both
private and public spending.

Finally, the social democratic strategy depended on cooperative
relations between workers and management made mutually bene-
ficial through sharing the rewards of an expanding economic economy. Unlike the case in the United States, most Swedish workers
were members of trade unions that bargained cooperatively with
corporations. But declining economic growth was undermining
worker–management cooperation. Myrdal insisted that Swedish
trade unions had always acted reasonably and were wise enough
not to be irresponsible in their demands for higher wages. He then
paused and added, "It is difficult to predict what will happen because of this terrible inflation."

The changed economic environment was affecting a key element
of Sweden's social democratic strategy. Myrdal acknowledged that,
when the economic pie was growing, Sweden had been able to provide its citizens with more social goods and services and still in-

crease private consumption. But when economic growth stagnates, public spending is not so readily accepted. Under those conditions it is difficult to sustain cooperation among different groups of workers when they must reduce their personal consumption. And how do you maintain Sweden's "solidaristic wage policy," which had been designed to reduce wage inequality? As Myrdal acknowledged, "It has become more difficult to ask a carpenter to accept a decline in his real wages while helping a textile worker earn a little more." He then paused and said, "It may be much more difficult to get people to care about each other."

I wondered what Sweden could do to repair these foundational problems. Sweden like other industrial countries was experiencing declines in some of its basic industries. Myrdal exclaimed, "Call it planning or not, in Sweden we are not prepared to follow the advice of Milton Friedman and just let those big industries crash. What we have done is subsidize those industries. With active government support, we brought firms together in larger complexes. It was a type of improvised planning that we will continue to do."

I asked what role workers should play in Sweden's economic planning. Did Sweden need to move beyond distributional socialism toward greater economic democracy? I alluded to a plan introduced by the Swedish labor economist Rudolf Meidner that would transfer a portion of corporate profits into a wage fund enabling trade unions to participate in investment decisions. Myrdal thought it was a good idea. "Profit," he exclaimed, "should be kept for investments. Say there is a recession. Should you ask workers to keep their wages down to prevent the decline in our progressive industries while profits are given to shareholders who don't play any economic role?"

But when I asked whether workers should have the right to participate in investment decisions, he hesitated. "How the hell are you going to get workers who live in comfortable houses, own automobiles, summer houses, perhaps motorboats, to take an active interest in—or have the knowledge to utilize—their democratic influence on the organization of industry? This is a real problem. Look, as standards of living rise, individuals have greater opportunities to take care of their own personal interests."

Half joking, I asked Myrdal if Sweden was creating a bourgeois ethic. Did the welfare state face what might be called "a paradox of success"?

He hesitated for a moment but then nodded and said, "In a society where the welfare state has been successful, you also create quite a bourgeois lifestyle." He lamented that Stockholm didn't have a single morning labor newspaper and some of the popular weeklies were frankly pornographic or were concerned about the Queen or other unimportant matters. Sweden, he said, faced other important problems that my questions ignored. He worried that alcoholism was becoming a real concern. It was common for young people to start drinking at the age of thirteen. That surprised me. I wondered why a country with an extensive social welfare system and full employment had problems no different from those in the United States.

Myrdal's explanation echoed the views of Senator Patrick Moynihan. "Our social problems," he said, "are related to the breakdown of the family. We are no different from Americans living in a different society." After a pause, he added, "This is not a question of socialism. Socialism, my friend, does not have the complete answer to every problem."

Folkheim, or "people's home," was a term sometimes used to describe Sweden's welfare state. It projected a vison of a harmonious society of equal citizens protected from the insecurities of modern capitalism. But Myrdal intimated that Sweden's utopian vision was fading. As workers became more affluent, they wanted to spend more of their income on personal consumption, limiting what could be used to meet the public goods necessary to strengthen the "people's home. " It seemed that Sweden had not discovered a way of sustaining the ethical foundation to maintain its *Folkheim*. Conversations with Swedish economists confirmed my sense that Sweden's efforts to build a middle way between socialism and capitalism faced significant challenges. The nation had made considerable progress toward creating a more just society but had not resolved the question of how much influence workers should have over production decisions.

I questioned whether social democrats could continue to construct a socially just society without expanding labor's participation in corporate investment decisions. Could Sweden's version of democratic capitalism survive without addressing the question of economic power? Capitalism depends on property rights—that is, vesting legal ownership over the means of production in individuals. Those rights were not widely distributed. The ownership of Swedish corporations was in fewer hands than in the United States. The Meidner Plan was introduced to counter the economic power of corporations.

The power problem continued to guide my conversations with

leading social democrats and trade unionists. How political and economic power influence decision making is rarely addressed in traditional economic analysis. Those discussions confirmed what was becoming more evident; the prospects for social reform were diminishing while free market ideology was playing a greater role in social and economic policy decisions. Myrdal's dismay upon learning that he would share the Nobel Prize in Economics with Frederick Hayek in 1974 was an early warning of the shifting political climate. At the time social democracy had entered a period of uncertainty. By the end of the 1980s the ideas of Hayek, not Myrdal, would increasingly guide economic policy in the United States and Great Britain.

After returning to New York, I contacted Gosta Rehn. He and Rudolph Meidner were senior Swedish trade union economists who had played a key role in designing Sweden's social democratic strategy. Rehn not only agreed to see me but asked if I could put him up for a few days so we could have more time to talk. Since I had only recently moved into my Brooklyn apartment, I told him that I wasn't ready to invite guests. But he shrugged off my concerns, and before long we were engrossed in many long conversations. Rehn clarified how Sweden was able to provide jobs for everyone and maintain price stability. The key was keeping enough slack in the economy to avoid inflation. Unemployment caused by declining aggregate demand was eliminated by government spending. The remaining structural unemployment was addressed by developing active labor policies to balance the demand and supply of workers' skills. This involved investments in worker training and in funds to help workers move to new locations to find jobs.

It was an innovative approach that depended on cooperation between Sweden's trade unions and corporations. But when economic expansion faded, divisions among workers and conflicts between workers and bosses erupted. In response to these conflicts, trade unions began to raise questions about the corporations' investment decisions, demanding a greater voice in how corporations used their profits.

I wondered whether Sweden should rely more on economic planning rather than the market to solve some of its current problems. Gosta thought words like "planning" and "control" were not the right response. To promote the more effective use of private investment required greater coordination and cooperation among corporations, municipal authorities, worker organizations, and even consumers. "Planning is like Hallelujah: It is not enough to sing it; you must do it."

"But," I asked, "shouldn't planning require greater democratic control over corporate investment decisions, greater economic democracy?"

Gosta smiled and said, "Yes, this would be desirable—but how to do it? How can the rat tie the bell around the neck of the cat?"

His skepticism didn't stop him from imagining new ways of expanding the welfare state. I was particularly interested in his plan to give workers greater control over their working time. Why he asked should workers have to wait until they retired to have more freedom over the uses of their time? Why shouldn't workers be permitted to draw on their future social security income to take sabbaticals to pursue new interests? I nodded in approval but asked why Sweden hadn't done more to reduce the hours of work.

"How can we do that," he said, "when workers were willing to work more to access middle-class consumption?" Keynes' vision about a workless future seemed as remote as ever.

In my conversation with the British economist Joan Robison, I found someone who spoke openly about the declining influence and power of social democracy. She had worked closely with John Maynard Keynes when he was developing his critique of traditional economic theory in the 1930s. In recent years she had become one of the foremost critics of traditional economic ideas. Many economists thought she deserved to be given the Nobel Prize in economics. They believed her rejection of standard economic theory prevented her from getting one.

I entered her Cambridge office in great anticipation. She had famously launched a battle with the other Cambridge dons, taking on such luminaries as the economist Paul Samuelson, whose textbook was used in most beginning college economic courses. And as a woman, she challenged the old boys club that dominated the economics profession.

Her warm greeting put me at ease, erasing any lingering anxiety I felt about our meeting. The woman who greeted me was in her early eighties and appeared somewhat frail. But she quickly revealed that she was as spirited and sharp in expressing her views about current affairs as I had imagined.

Given the more conservative turn in the British Labor Party, I was particularly interested in Robinson's views about the British welfare state. Labor's radical programs of the early 1970s had waned. Earlier efforts to create a "public enterprise economy" had been shelved. The plan would have, under government supervision, harnessed the power of large corporations and initiated greater worker participation in economic planning. Subsequent labor governments abandoned the left's social reform programs. Stuart Holland, a labor member of Parliament, told me that labor governments had introduced conservative monetarist policies, cut public spending, and restrained trade unions rather than transform the large corporations.

I asked Joan whether she thought the British welfare state was in crisis. Shaking her head, she grimly responded, "In this country the idea of the welfare state has been abandoned by the government, and what we're having is a class war made from above, a class war by the rich against the poor." Encouraged by her forthright response, I asked how this had happened. What was unfolding, she said, was partly a response to trade union actions, which she thought not strategically wise but primarily a consequence of a declining economic pie and the scrambling over what's left to share.

I wondered whether those problems were a consequence of the success of Keynesian economic policy. I suggested that, in the aftermath of the Second World War, Britain had periodically experienced high levels of employment and free collective bargaining between a strong labor movement and a concentrated business sector. Britain's success had generated expectations of expanding real income for everybody. I asked whether that created problems even for a labor government. "Is full employment and free collective bargaining," I asked, "compatible with price stability and balance of payments equilibrium?"

She responded sharply. "But it wasn't *real* stability. Look, for twenty years after the war, I used to say our situation is like the man falling from a skyscraper. As he passed the 14th floor he called out, 'It's not too bad so far.' It was a boom, and it had many of the characteristic of a boom, among which was that it wouldn't last. But then, of course, history always catches you out—for example, the oil crisis. But even before the oil crisis, the scarcity of many crucial materials had begun to develop. It couldn't last. Many people succumbed to the idea that capitalism had changed, and it was going to be all right. That was a self-interested reaction on the part of the haves saying to the have-nots, 'What are you complaining about?'"

Our conversation turned on efforts to address problems of inflation and economic stagnation. When I asked her about monetarist solutions to address these difficult economic problems, her response echoed those of Myrdal. "Monetarism is a lot of nonsense. It's just mistaking a symptom for a cause. Monetarists say that too much money is being created. If less money is created, then prices won't rise so fast. It's just silly. And they have this idea that there is a big difference between spending by government and by business. Expenditures by government are presumed to be inflationary. That's just superstition."

I asked whether the motivation behind monetarist policies to deflate the economy was connected to their objective of reducing the power of labor. "Yes," she said. "It was very evident in Great Britain—the attack on the trade unions and the welfare state. This country has always been very class-ridden. By broadening the base of our educational system, we were struggling a little bit to change that class divide. Now we've gone right back on it. People use slogans to conceal from themselves what they're doing. But it's almost a conscious class war of the rich against the poor."

The unequal distribution of income and wealth was of particular concern. "Look," she said, "the hierarchy of incomes—-who gets what? That's the one subject the ordinary person is most interested in. Orthodox economic theory, based on the defense of laissez-faire, claims that it is efficient. But according to their own doctrine, these big differences in income are not efficient. Sixpence to a poor man is more than sixpence to a rich man. Some people take pills for indigestion while others are starving. They're caught in this contradiction that their precious laissez-faire is inefficient."

Her despair about addressing Britain's economic ills was palpable. When I said that socialists no longer had faith in the efficiency of economic planning, she responded that socialists hadn't reckoned sufficiently with the problems of uncertainty and bureaucracy. She added, "It's very difficult to be on the side of freedom on the one hand, and on the side of order on the other hand. It's a perennial problem." But when I asked how she reconciled those conflicting goals, she shook her head and said, "I'm not God."

I persisted, though. I asked if she had the authority what would she do to address Britain's current economic problems.

"Well," she said, "you could try to radically redistribute wealth, but then you're going to get your head cut off in the process. How are you going to do it without busting the system?"

"Should you bust the system?" I asked.

"The system will bust you," she said dismissively. "Just because I studied economics, do you think I'm the archangel Gabriel who can straighten everything out? I'm very old and I've lived through a lot of history. And I find it very disappointing."

"We seem to keep getting back to the question of economic power," I responded.

"If we could solve that problem," she said, "we'd be in a different world."

Joan Robinson's pessimism should not have surprised me. The political climate had changed. Keynes' visionary prediction of a radically reformed capitalist society had faded. As the 1980s unfolded it was Friedrich Hayek's utopian version of market fundamentalism that would capture the political zeitgeist.

Chapter 7

THE WANING OF UTOPIAN HOPE

N THE EARLY 1980S MY PERSONAL and political world was in flux. My marriage of twenty-nine years had ended. The radicalism of the 1960s and 1970s had faded, and labor's power continued its long decline. A renewed faith in market fundamentalism challenged the New Deal consensus that had guided American politics. The neo-Liberal belief in the free market became the dominant ideology guiding American politics at the same time as the collapse of Soviet Union in 1991 ended a revolution that had inspired my mother's fantasies and a little boy's belief in new ways of living. For the defenders of unfettered capitalism, the fall of communism confirmed their view that the socialist vision was, as Hayek proclaimed, a "fatal conceit." But Mikhail Gorbachev's initial efforts to reform the Soviet economy and society rekindled hopes that the Soviet Union might become a more democratic socialist society.

It was an historic moment that offered an opportunity to witness the transformation of a revolution that was for many the defining event of the 20th century.

In the winter of 1990, I travelled to Moscow to organize a conversation between Russian intellectuals, trade union leaders, and their American counterparts about Soviet efforts to transform its economy and society. By focusing on the "labor problem" I hoped to challenge the commonly held belief that free market principles could be quicky used to guide the transformation of the Soviet economy. In those early stages of Soviet economic reform, I believed the Soviet Union had the possibility of creating a social democratic society. Those hopes would quickly fade.

On a cold winter morning in 1990 our plane landed in Leningrad, soon to revert to St. Petersburg, its pre-Soviet name. It was the first leg of our trip to Moscow. Mike Yanowitch and I had come to Leningrad at the invitation of Robert Vogt, Hofstra University's dean, to participate in discussions about developing a branch campus in Leningrad. I was invited in part because of my experience in creating Hofstra's campus in Manhattan.

As I walked out of the airport to a waiting car, I felt a surge of excitement and apprehension. The Soviet Union had loomed so large in my life. While I had long rejected my childhood illusions about it, my memories of Soviet resistance to fascism during the Second World War still stirred my imagination when I joined my friends in singing, "Fly higher and higher and higher, our emblem is the Soviet Star." Now, I could see for myself what the Soviet Union was really like. Well, Mom, I thought, here I am in the country of your dreams and illusions.

Our meeting with Soviet political and economic officials was scheduled for the evening. We were driven to a compound outside the center of the city that the Communist Party used for special meetings and events. The grounds, even while still covered with snow, were quite beautiful. We were housed in a large cottage with several rooms that were modestly furnished but certainly adequate. Whatever the special perks that Soviet communist leaders received, they were not on display in that Communist Party retreat.

Later that evening we were driven to a restaurant and ushered into a small private dining room where our hosts were already seated. I had read about the Soviet nomenclature. Here they were in full display. Present were managers of firms, local government officials, a few high-ranking military officers, and some university professors. I had a momentary feeling of déjà vu as the meal progressed and the vodka began to flow. But unlike my experience with the North Korean delegation in Cuba, I resisted our hosts' efforts to get me intoxicated.

I did not realize at the time that I was witnessing the beginning of the devolution of Soviet communism. It was my first glimpse of its leaders seeking to reap personal benefits from Gorbachev's political and economic reforms. *Glasnost* and *perestroika* were designed to provide greater opportunity for the free exchange of ideas, and to loosen central control over the economy. But Gorbachev had underestimated the corruption and self-interest of the Soviet nomenclature as they began to respond to the weakening of Communist Party control over the economy and society.

As the conversation unfolded, I became increasingly suspicious of the Soviet officials' motivations and goals. They spoke about reforms and changes in the Soviet economy and society, and about the necessity of training a new generation of business leaders. They hoped that Hofstra University would be willing to create a branch campus in Leningrad to train Soviet managers to meet new economic challenges. It was a large-scale undertaking. I wondered whether they had the resources and political capital to undertake such an ambitious project.

But change was in the air, and there was something seductive about participating such a moment of radical change in Soviet society.

The next day we were driven to a large building that overlooked the Baltic Sea, and we were told that the five-story building (then used as a vocational high school) could be restructured to house the Hofstra University Business School.

After a quick tour of the building, I asked my colleagues what they thought these Soviet bureaucrats hoped to personally gain from the ambitious undertaking. Their motives soon became more transparent when, almost as an afterthought, the managers of a local China Wear factory said, "If we move forward with this important project, we hope that our children will be able to attend Hofstra University tuition free."

Nothing ever materialized from these discussions. It was not until we arrived in Moscow that it became more apparent that the Soviet Union was undergoing radical political and economic changes. Over the next ten years I would witness the rapid devolution of the Soviet Union and the disturbing choices Russia would make in its transition to capitalism.

Mike and I walked into Tat'iana Zaslavskaia's office with great anticipation. Mike had edited several of her books. She was a distinguished sociologist and an intellectual force in the Soviet social reform movement. Her public opinion surveys provided important information about the changing attitudes and beliefs of ordinary people as they experienced the radical transformation of the Soviet economy and society. She was a tall woman, large in frame but with a soft and inviting voice. Zaslavskaia smiled broadly as she invited us to our seats. She began to speak to Mike in Russian, acknowledging his help in publishing some of her articles, but quickly shifted to English to be sure that I was engaged in the conversation.

As she began to respond to our plans to organize a Soviet–U.S. conference, I found myself drawn to the sound of her voice and her mannerism. They seemed so familiar. I suddenly realized that she reminded me of my mother. I was afraid to speak. It was not unlike that moment in Cuba when Carlos Raphael Rodriguez confirmed my views about Cuba's economic problems and illusions. With great difficulty I succeeded in suppressing those feelings and began raising some general questions about the problems the Soviets faced.

Tat'iana was part of a group of Soviet intellectuals who supported a gradual transition to a more social democratic society but was uncertain where the road to reform might lead. While her surveys revealed general support for Gorbachev's efforts, popular support could only be assured if the promise of a better life for ordinary people could be realized. I did not anticipate that, on December 25, 1991, the Soviet Union would cease to exist—marking what Eric Hobsbawm called the end of the short 20th century. Nor did I foresee that Russia would rely on market fundamentalism to guide its radical transformation to capitalism.

In the summer of 2012, I recall turning to a Chinese urban planner seated next to me in a restaurant in Beijing, commenting on the remarkable progress his country was making in rapidly modernizing their economy and how different their economic transition has been from what I had encountered in Russia. He smiled and asked if I had read Charles Dickens. "China," he said, "is experiencing the best of times and the worst of times." In 1997 few ordinary people in Russia would have offered even such hedged assurances.

But that was not true of some prominent American economists who were certain that Russia had been regenerated. I wondered what evidence the Harvard economist Martin Feldstein had for exclaiming in the Summer of 1997 that Russia had been reborn and could now look forward to a bright new future. Russia's rapid privatization of its economy was, in his words, "one of the most remarkable achievements of the twentieth century." In sharp contrast to his optimistic vision, I saw a Russia deeply divided between a new rich and a growing, struggling new poor. It seemed clear to me that Russia had taken the wrong road in its efforts to create a modern capitalist economy.

Was I being too pessimistic? Leonid Gordon thought I needed a broader historical perspective. He was convinced that Russia was going through a phase of economic and social development that the United States had already been through. "Bert," he said, "Russia is experiencing its version of 'wild-West capitalism' that your country experienced in the late 19th century".

"No, Leonid," I responded, "Russia is reaping the consequences of its reliance on neo-liberal ideas to guide its transition to capitalism—with devastating results."

There was something familiar about Russia's efforts to quickly transform its economy. It had the ring of the Bolshevik ideology that had guided the Soviet economic system. The communist Bolsheviks, like its neo-liberal reformers, believed that scientific economic principles guided their policies. Both viewed themselves as an enlightened vanguard whose top-down efforts to destroy the old order should be quickly imposed. Like the Bolsheviks, they viewed the pain their policies inflicted on the Russian people as a necessary part of building a prosperous future. And they too believed that there was no alternative to their economic strategy to rapidly develop a modern capitalist society.

Whatever hope I had that Russia might choose a more democratic socialist path quickly faded. Market bolshevism's embrace of what became known as the "Washington Consensus" asserted that countries with the most open and free domestic and foreign trade markets would be the most successful in making the necessary structural adjustment to compete in the new global economy. Embracing the neo-liberal playbook, Russia quickly privatized the economy, liberalized prices, and implemented tough fiscal and monetary policies, expecting that flexible and free markets would do the rest. They were mistaken.

In our book *New Rich New Poor New Russia: Winners and Losers on the Russian Road to Capitalism*, Mike and I exposed the consequences of Russia's failed economic strategy. Workers' living standards declined sharply, generating feelings of economic and social insecurity that workers had not experienced under communism. By the beginning of 1999 thirty-eight percent of Russians were living in poverty. Life expectancy, especially for men, dropped dramatically. And a new economic elite emerged from the ashes of the old communist order.

Russia dampened my hopes for a *besser velt*. Yet there were moments that reawakened childhood dreams. I remember an evening I spent sharing a meal of chicken drumsticks—a gift from President George H.W. Bush to help Russians after the collapse of communism. Seated around a large table with an extended Jewish family ranging in age from the mid-90s to young children, I smiled in recognition as they debated the consequences of Russian economic policies. The conversation was conducted in English and Russian and, at times, in Yiddish. It reminded me of my large family gatherings when we passionately debated how to reform American society. Clearly, communist repression had not extinguished this Jewish family's critical thinking and their aspirations for a better life.

Discouraged by what I had observed in Russia, I hoped Sweden might still offer a viable alternative to the increasing influence of neo-liberal social and economic policies. In the Spring of 1997, I had an opportunity to meet Rudolf Meidner, who had played a leading role in developing Sweden's social democratic policies. Yvonne Hirdman, a Swedish historian and friend of Alice, introduced me to Meidner. In the days that followed, I encountered a man deeply troubled about the future of social democracy.

Meidner greeted me warmly when we met on a sunny day in Stockholm. Smiling he commented that he enjoyed reading my interview with his friend and collaborator Gosta Rehn. I laughed and said, "That was so long ago. In those conversations, Gosta expressed confidence in the enduring strength of Sweden's social democratic model."

"Yes," Meidner responded, "Gosta wanted to put a positive spin on Sweden's hopes and possibilities. At that time, we thought we could still resolve some of the problems Sweden was facing."

He lamented that Sweden had failed to address a key problem in the Swedish economic model. Under Sweden's solidaristic wage policy, originally known as the socialist wage policy, workers doing the same work were paid the same wages regardless of the firm's profitability, size, or location. As a result of the wage constraints exercised by well-paid workers, more efficient firms began earning excess profits. He explained how Sweden tried to address this problem by introducing a plan that would transfer part of the "forfeited" wage increases of the more skilled workers into a collective wage-earner fund. This was a way of sharing the excess profits that had accumulated because of trade union wage constraints. The wage-earner fund would provide a mechanism for greater trade union participation in corporate investment decision. But, he lamented, the Social Democratic party did not endorse the idea, and it never became part of the Swedish model.

In conversations that followed it became more evident that Meidner had lost faith in Sweden's ability to solve the current problems of Swedish social democracy. He spoke about the failure of the Swedish government efforts in the second half of the 1980s to deal effectively with the problems of an overheated economy.

"But what about now?" I responded. "Unemployment has risen to 8 percent. The solidaristic wage policy had been almost abandoned, and welfare-state programs I am told were being cut back."

Meidner hesitated before responding. "Look," he said, "the Swedish Model is not working. By some measures unemployment has risen to 15 percent of the labor force. The goal of equality has been undermined but not quite as clearly. You can see the widening gap between different groups, even between men and women. You can say that equality is no longer one of its main goals. But the welfare system has not broken down."

In the days that followed, our conversation continued to range over a variety of problems that Sweden and Western capitalist economies were confronting. He lamented that the Swedish government was trying to follow the new ideology of low budget deficits to achieve price stability. "You cannot do this," he insisted, "and at the same time achieve full employment." I could sense his pessimism. "Sweden is a small country," he said, "and we cannot neglect international reactions to domestic economic policies. We are losing part of our manufacturing industry in the search for lower labor costs, and yet the Social Democratic party is unwilling to give trade unions additional power to influence the uses of corporate investments."

"This is puzzling," I said. "Why, in a country where 85 percent of the workforce is unionized, hasn't the labor movement been able to mobilize its members to change social democratic policies?"

"They are unwilling to do it because they are afraid to start a debate about the wage-earner funds. And in Sweden workers are passive."

"What," I asked, "will it take to revitalize the social democratic movement?"

He shrugged. "It will take a long time, maybe a generation."

"Why so long?"

"Because people must experience the total failure of the present system. It must be felt by almost everyone that the current neo-liberal approach does not work. But it is still working. Capital is dominant."

"Rudolf," I countered, "what do you mean by the total failure of the system?"

His response still troubles me. "There are different ways it could fail. It could be very painful. Economic problems could lead to a fascist dictatorship."

"So," I responded, "in the short run you are very pessimistic about reviving the social democratic model?"

"Yes," he said. "You must go through a very painful period. You see signs of it already in a country like Sweden. We are excluding large groups of people. Immigrants are living under very difficult conditions. And our long-term unemployed are excluded from what life should give people. The gaps are widening. Solidarity is just a word that is used in pronouncements but is not realized." His pessimism was unsettling.

"Rudolf," I asked, "aren't there new voices capable of countering these challenges to social democracy?"

His answer continues to resonate. "Don't ask an old man. There is a risk that I cannot hear these new voices, but that is dangerous. Many of them are nonsocialist concepts taken over from neo-classical ideology. Bert, I must be careful not to be too pessimistic. It was easier for us. We had the privilege of living at a time when we had goals and the possibilities to achieving them. It was a very exceptional moment in Sweden. We were on the way to achieving these splendid goals of solidarity, of equal opportunity, of general welfare, of high employment, so everyone could be free to choose. And the economic system was efficient and competitive. Of course, there is a risk that my memory is not so clear. But these were the best decades, and you will not get them back so easily. Bert, you asked if there were people with new ideas. I don't see them today. But maybe that's my fault."

In the Spring of 1998 Alice was invited by President Clinton to give a keynote address celebrating advances in women's citizenship. I stood next to her, waiting to be greeted by the President. I was told I could only exchange a few words with him when he approached. When he finally stood before me, I handed him my Russian book and exclaimed, "Mr. President, Russia taught me that a key principle of successful social policy is the importance of rewarding the losers."

He thumbed through my book before responding and then,

Nodding, said, "Yes, I believe that." Was he being disingenuous? He did not act on those values when he boldly exclaimed that he was "ending welfare as we know it."

My utopian dreams had diminished. The 20th century was ending. Political engagement in the struggle to build a more equal society had faded. An expanding middle class strove to secure its social and economic position in a changing post-industrial society. Competition for limited-quality living space and education was inflicting increasing financial and psychological stress on families and their children. Trade union membership continued to decline as workers struggled to find secure jobs in an economy experiencing rapid changes in the recipe of production and globalization. Workers affected by changes in work requirements and in racial and sexual norms were turning away from the Democratic Party, many embracing a radical right ideology. Hopes for reviving social democratic values were fading.

In November 2016 Donald Trump was elected President of the United States. His election exposed the fragility of American democracy. In defeating Hillary Clinton, Trump exploited entrenched cultural, racial, and economic divisions, igniting deep-seated antidemocratic sentiments. Only eight years earlier America had elected its first Black president. Charismatic, articulate, and engaging, Obama's presidency might have ushered in a new era of cultural and economic reform. Coming at a time of economic crisis, I hoped Obama would respond quickly by enacting New Deal-type economic reforms and begin addressing America's growing income and wealth disparities. I was wrong.

Instead, Obama responded with a smaller set of emergency measures that, while stabilizing the economy, launched a period of slow economic growth that left many workers resentful and disillusioned. His economic recovery program benefited more educated middle-income groups but left large segments of the white working class behind while corporations got bigger and economic power became more concentrated.

Why, I wondered, didn't he try to mobilize the American people who had elected him rather than wasting his political capital vainly attempting to convince a resistant Republican party to support his legislative agenda? While he succeeded in expanding health care and enlarged the regulation of the economy, he appeared weak when he tried to negotiate with his adversaries. In failing to reach out to workers threatened by the changing demands of a post-industrial economy, he set the stage for the rise of white working-class resentment fueled by a Trump presidency.

On a sunny afternoon in September 2011, my Irish son-in-law and I joined a large crowd shouting "We are the ninety-nine percent!"

I spotted my friends the philosopher Nancy Fraser and historian Eli Zaretsky moving toward us shouting, "Isn't this wonderful?"

I laughed, yelling, "The people, yes!"

Nancy seemed uncertain. "I'm not sure about the ninety-nine percent."

"It's perfect." I said. "They're trying to organize a broad-based popular movement that includes affluent academics like us."

But the spark that ignited those protests soon faded. The encampment set up in Zuccotti Park in Lower Manhattan attracted radical tourists, but the protests gradually ended. Other social movements surfaced, inspiring new protests for gender and racial justice. I joined the Women's March on Washington and participated in the historic Black Lives Matter demonstrations. Yet something had changed. My hopes and dreams for a better world seemed ever more distant.

Epilogue

MY UTOPIAN IMAGINATION

O N A WARM, SUNNY AUGUST DAY, I gathered with family and friends in our Berkshire house to celebrate my 90th and Alice's 80th birthday. Holding hands, she and I blew out the many candles on our birthday cake to cheers and the singing of "You have a birthday, we have none, we sing to you." When the screaming and laughing ended, I felt an inexplicable desire to share with my loved ones an alternative vision to our current way of living.

"I finally went to the mountaintop," I told my family. "And I found the elderly sage I've been looking for all my life." That captured everyone's attention as I began to speak about my utopian dreams. "I'm not sure I fully grasped everything the sage revealed, but I want to share with you what he believed were the prerequisites for living a liberated life. He began with a warning. "I can disclose what you need to do," he said, "but it will be very difficult to implement. You must imagine a world no longer dominated by the money motive and the costly competition for social and economic standing. But you have reached a level of economic development that makes it possible to realize a vision of new ways of living."

And then, to my surprise, he asked if I had listened carefully to the words of the Rolling Stones when they sang about not always getting what you want but what you need. He said, "People must learn to want less, to get what they need. This is the first principle for achieving a liberated life." He acknowledged how difficult it will be to change our consumer culture because corporate profits depend on creating an ever-expanding demand for consumer goods. But he insisted that, until we begin to consume less, we will not be able to fulfill the second condition for leading an emancipated life.

He then paused for a moment, signaling the importance of the second principle. "To be truly free, you must gain greater control over the uses of your time. In the pursuit of profits, bosses have resisted reducing working time with disturbing consequences for family life, civil society, and nature itself. You have been seduced into consuming more rather than working less. Until that changes, you will never be able to gain control over how you use your time. Karl Marx was not alone in imagining a period when workers would be able to determine how they spend their days and nights. John Maynard Keynes also predicted, almost a century ago, that you would need to work no more than fifteen hours a week to meet your needs."

The sage reminded me of Keynes' stinging words about what would be necessary to gain control over the uses of our labor. He envisioned a time in the future when the accumulation of wealth would no longer be of great social importance and when there would be great changes in our moral code. We would then be able "to afford to dare to assess the money motive at its true value. The love of money as a possession—as distinguished from the love of money as means of enjoyments and realities of life—will be recognized for what it is, a somewhat disgusting morbidity, one of those semi-criminal, semi-pathological propensities which one hands over with a shudder to the specialists in mental disease."

I had paused for a moment, trying to gather my thoughts, when someone shouted, "What's the third condition?" Laughing, I grasped Alice's hand and replied, "He proclaimed that love conquers all." Everyone began hooting and shouting. "Wait!" I said. "Do you really believe that love and benevolence could replace self-interest as the primary motive guiding our decisions and actions?" I wanted to say more but hesitated. It wasn't the time for such a conversation.

I had always been critical of the economist's reliance on self-interest as the underlying force that drove individual behavior. It was Adam Smith who proclaimed that we get our daily bread, not from our benevolence, from our self-interest. It became a central principle of economics that society was more secure when it was built on the pursuit of self-interest. Yet it seems to me that, when capitalism dispenses with love or civic virtue, it loses its vitality and stability.

Love is not like any other scarce resource whose supply decreases with use. As the economist Albert Hirschman noted, the availability and quality of love increases rather than decreases with use. Love or civic virtue, like playing a musical instrument or maintaining proficiency in a new language, decline when not used. But as I witnessed in Cuba, civic engagement can be wasted when it is seen as costless and not carefully nurtured. Love may not be enough to create the conditions of a good society, but it is an essential ingredient for building a liberated society.

Are those dreams just illusions? Is the struggle to create a better world a necessary part of our destiny? Albert Camus leaves Sisyphus at the foot of the mountain as he begins his ascent. There is no false god or ideology to help him. He must push his rock by his own efforts. Is that our fate? Is the struggle for a better life itself enough to fill our hearts? Is Camus too utopian in imagining Sisyphus happy.

These are ominous times. I am reminded of Meidner's warning of troubling years ahead. I resist acquiescing to gloomy predictions about the future. It's my father's, not my mother's, voice that keeps resounding in my thoughts. It provides some consolation. I can see him standing before a large Jewish audience singing in Yiddish. "It may be that I have built my castles in the sky / In my dreams it is brighter, in my dreams it is better, in my dreams the sky is bluer than blue" *(In troym iz mir heler, in troym iz mire besser, in kholem der Himmel iz bluer fun bloy").*